Leading Churches
Through Change

Leading Churches Through Change

Douglas Alan Walrath

Creative Leadership Series
Lyle E. Schaller, Editor

Abingdon / Nashville

LEADING CHURCHES THROUGH CHANGE

Library of Congress Cataloging in Publication Data

WALRATH, DOUGLAS ALAN, 1933–
  Leading churches through change.
  (Creative leadership series)
  1. Church growth—Case studies. 2. Pastoral theology—Case studies.
  I. Title.
  BV652.25.W34   254'.5   79-4456

ISBN 0-687-21270-7

MANUFACTURED BY THE PARTHENON PRESS AT
NASHVILLE, TENNESSEE, UNITED STATES OF AMERICA

Foreword

Perhaps the most effective means of encouraging congregational leaders to evaluate the role and goals of their own church is to encourage them to visit similar congregations and to reflect on what they see and hear. This is not always easy! Sometimes it is difficult to identify similar congregations with parallel concerns. Frequently, it is difficult to schedule the visit and motivate the leaders to invest the time, money, and energy for such a trip. Often the parallels are less than obvious, and therefore it is difficult to extract the most significant lessons from the visit.

An alternative approach for these congregational leaders is to study a collection of case studies. In this volume, Douglas Alan Walrath has described six real-life congregations, plus one cluster arrangement. He details the changes, opportunities, problems, challenges, and frustrations encountered by the people in each setting. He walks along beside the members of the congregations as they respond in different ways to the challenges of change. In a remarkably sympathetic and understanding style, he enables the reader both to see and to feel the responses of real people, as they are faced with difficult and frustration-producing choices. At the end of each chapter, the author points out the lessons that can be extracted from these experiences. In the final chapter, he outlines a series of leadership principles that will be helpful to creative church leaders everywhere.

If one were to lift up the most unique contribution of this volume, it would be Doug's review of the Palatine Cluster, a cooperative venture involving five congregations on the rural-urban fringe. This absorbing, candid, and instructive account should be required reading for anyone with either a participatory or an academic interest in clustering arrangements!

A basic assumption in this book, as in the earlier volumes of the Creative Leadership Series, is that creative church leaders can profit from the experiences, insights, and wisdom accumulated by leaders in other congregations. In this volume, Doug Walrath offers the reader a fascinating series of insights and lessons gleaned from the victories and the defeats of committed congregational leaders, as they sought to be faithful and obedient to a common Lord.

Through these case studies, lay leaders, pastors, and seminarians can learn from the experiences of a variety of congregations that have been confronted with the pressures of change.

How can this book and the earlier volumes in this series be used most creatively? A growing number of congregations are selecting one of these volumes as a study book for the members of the governing board. In a typical procedure, the monthly meeting begins with a brief devotional period, followed by a fifteen- to thirty-minute discussion of a chapter in one of the books. Then the members turn to the regular business agenda. Is that approach a possibility for your congregation? This volume could be the book used to initiate that practice.

Lyle E. Schaller
Yokefellow Institute

Contents

Preface

This book is about real people in real congregations, who sometimes win and sometimes lose, who sometimes thrive and sometimes barely survive amidst the changes that characterize our time. The events in the case studies which follow actually happened, most of them within the last five or six years, all of them within the last decade. I know firsthand every situation I describe. I have changed the names and locations and other identifying details to save some from possible embarrassment.

This is not a book of success stories. In the real world, there are as many defeats as there are victories. In fact, there are more defeats. Most of the time, no one talks about the defeats. This is unfortunate! In my experience, we can learn as much, sometimes more, from our failures, as from our successes—if we are willing. During my years as a church planner and researcher, I have attempted many innovations. Most were only moderately successful, or, to put it bluntly, many were failures. But I am able to put into practice in my day-to-day work the leadership principles I learned from those failures. So while the failures were real, they were not losses. I profited from them immensely.

Each chapter begins with a case study of typical dilemmas through which local leaders have had to make their way, followed by an analysis pointing out principles of leadership that those involved either utilized or failed to employ. The first two chapters deal with a challenge many church leaders face in our time: community decline. Well over half the churches of our country are located in rural or city areas that have seen heavy economic and social loss over the last several decades. In order to survive, these congregations must find means to carry on their ministries with significantly fewer resources.

Chapter 1 is a study of Stephentown, a small, rural village church that grows and thrives, contrary to the overall pattern of decline in rural congregations. With the help of some excellent resourcing by denominational leaders, this congregation is able to find superb and appropriate pastoral leadership, to develop program that successfully attracts new members, and then to integrate these new members into its core church life.

Chapter 2 is a study of two mergers, each designed to make one strong church out of two weak churches. However, the first merger, Winchester, actually results in the loss of most of the members of one of the original congregations, and continues to weaken the survivor. Church leaders here fail to take into account the very different social groups that compose these two congregations. Also, the process leading up to this merger is poorly planned, and even more poorly guided, by a pastor whose goals and values are out of step with the local communities and churches.

The other merger I describe in this chapter results in a church significantly stronger than either of the two that compose it. In this instance, social groups in the two merging congregations are very similar. Also, the process leading up to the merger is well-planned and very well-facilitated by lay leaders, and by the pastor who served both congregations immediately prior to the merger.

In the next two chapters, I explore another difficult challenge: finding effective ministry amidst social diversity. The widespread mobility of our time often brings two or more very different social groups face to face within the same congregation. This happens, for example, on the metropolitan fringe, when established congregations are overrun with suburban residents in new housing developments. The latter often seek a life-style and church program much different from that which the natives have supported. Congregations find great difficulty integrating the two groups and programming for them. Chapter 3 focuses on Elmwood, a former rural village now experiencing the pain of becoming suburban. Initially, old-timers welcome newcomers to their church. Then they discover that the newcomers, who at first sight appeared to be willing to support the status quo, actually want a different church experience. A new pastor misreads the natives' willingness to include newcomers. As his efforts to reach the new people are successful, the natives fear the newcomers' desire for change will undermine their traditional way of church life. They withdraw their support. Newcomers lose interest when the church does not relate positively to their needs and interests. The pastor then finds he is unable to carry on a successful ministry with either group.

Chapter 4 presents the Palatine Cluster, a cluster-team ministry among five metropolitan fringe congregations, which results both in benefits and surprising costs for the participants. Benefits include a cluster program that attracts many new persons, greater economic and administrative efficiency for the congregations, and a shared and rewarding team ministry for the pastors. Surprising costs include the inability to integrate those attracted by cluster programs into membership in any of the congregations, more investment than gain for two of the congregations, and much greater difficulty in maintaining a shared ministry than the pastors had anticipated.

The next two chapters present cases which describe the difficulty of finding an appealing church style in a consumer society. The past twenty or thirty years have led Americans to believe that their needs *deserve* to be met. People socialized in such a consumer society expect a church to meet their particular needs and interests. In order to thrive, a congregation, whether it is a new church or simply finds itself faced with a new group in its immediate neighborhood, needs to shape its program and life-style to speak specifically to those people now available to it.

Chapter 5 focuses on Newton, a little church that didn't make it—although in the beginning everybody thought it would. The founding pastor in this new church development field has that certain charisma which seems bound to appeal. He moves quickly to develop a "primary group" congregation. The church grows rapidly. Then, unexpectedly, its growth stops; years pass, and it is unable to move beyond a hundred-member limit. Close scrutiny reveals key misjudgments: all decision-making within the church depends on the pastor; the church's lack of formal organization limits the ability of most church members to assume leadership; many people in this high-mobility suburb are unwilling to enter into the intimacy which characterizes the congregation—the costs of leaving are too great. Though a valid concept, church as an intimate primary group turns out to be inappropriate for this suburban context.

Chapter 6 describes Wilmington Street, a city neighborhood church that discovers unanticipated potential. After years of steadily losing members, the church begins to grow. A surprising proportion of younger adults are among those who join. The church's planning committee senses a new opportunity, but is concerned about significant differences in life-style between newcomers and longtime members. It invites a denominational researcher to conduct a neighborhood analysis and to interview newcomers to discover their feeling about the congregation. His report confirms that a growing number of young adults are moving into the neighborhood. However, he discovers key differences between newcomers and longstanding church members; also, that the newcomers feel welcome, but not included or integrated into the congregation's life. The church's planning committee is able to develop program aimed at the specific needs of the new persons, and to plan means for their entry into the core life of the congregation.

Chapter 7 is a summary, highlighting the general leadership principles that emerge from the six cases.

Finally, some deserved words of gratitude. First of all, I thank the Synod of Albany that supported me when I was little known and knew little. I am grateful to colleagues at the Northeastern

Regional Center who, too often, I am afraid, carried more than their share of the load.

More recently I am indebted to the Lilly Endowment, whose funds supported me during a very significant six months of reflection, and especially to Robert Lynn.

During the past ten years, I have steadily grown in my appreciation of Jean Deere, who has helped clarify my ideas, as well as prepare the results of numerous research projects for publication, including some earlier versions of material that appears in this book. Janet Reid has demonstrated repeatedly how invaluable a research assistant can be. She also typed the entire final draft of this book. Herm Luben has helped to insure that most of my grammatical disorders are only temporary.

Also, I want to thank Lyle Schaller, whose open faith and quiet goading encouraged me to think I had something to say, and then to go ahead and write it down.

Finally, I thank Martha, my wife, and Martha Kay, Philip, Stephen, and Rebecca, my children, for living with me through all of it.

I. A Little Church Discovers a Big Potential

Introduction

Stephentown is a rural village located in an economically depressed county in the northeastern United States. The county borders the region the U.S. government has defined as Appalachia. For several decades, the general pattern of the county has been one of loss. The township surrounding Stephentown contains not quite half as many persons as it did fifty years ago. Economic loss parallels the loss of people. Looking from 1960 back to 1950, the number employed on farms in Stephentown's county, for example, dropped by one-third. That same rate of descent held through the 60s and 70s. As a consequence of the loss of job opportunities, most of the county's talented and imaginative young adults now leave the area to find employment. A continuing decline in self-esteem and political power has accompanied the economic loss and dwindling population. Its location, some distance from any metropolitan area, seriously limits Stephentown's potential for recovery.

The four Protestant churches in the village all struggle to survive. One has a parttime pastor; two share a pastor with another community. The congregation that is the focus of this chapter decided to attempt a recovery by widening its ministry.

Its successful development, facilitated by skilled lay and pastoral leadership and effective judicatory support, illustrates the surprising potential for survival and growth inherent in many small congregations.

The Case

In many ways, Pastor Jim Richards is one of the most unspectacular persons I have ever met. He isn't tall. He doesn't appear particularly intelligent. Most of the time he doesn't have a lot of say. Yet the results of his ministry are very impressive. On this ordinary Sunday morning, nearly one hundred fifty persons had gathered to worship. The number was not unusual; typically, this church has more persons attending Sunday morning worship than it has enrolled members.

The composition of the congregation is as outstanding as its size. On this particular Sunday, there were old people, to be sure, but also a surprising number of children, and an even more surprising number of young adults. Some worshipers were dressed in their Sunday best, while others did not appear to be dressed up at all.

At the coffee hour following worship, I shook hands with rough hands and smooth hands. I listened to those who were very articulate, and to those who had great difficulty expressing themselves. I talked with those who looked straight at me with healthy, happy eyes, and with those who were unable to return my gaze. It was a very mixed group. But to a person, they felt comfortable, included, and able to be together in this church.

Later, when the others had left, I asked Jim Richards how this particular rural congregation had become so unusual. He told me this story.

It really began a half dozen years ago in the parsonage kitchen in my former parish. Our conference executive came to visit me.

"Jim," he said, "I have a dream, and I want you to be a part of that dream. We have dozens of churches like the one you're in, in our conference. Across the country there are thousands more, all struggling to stay alive and slowly watching their lives slip away. Our conference, like most church judicatories, tries to keep them going by giving them all a little bit of help. You and I know that help has not been enough. Most of them are slowly but surely dying.

"For some months, I've been working with our conference Church Planning Committee to find a way to help our rural churches not only to survive, but to find an effective ministry. As you well know, that's not easy these days. For the last several decades, most of the rural areas of our country have experienced loss after loss after loss. Huge numbers of persons have left the family farms; young people grow up, go away to school and never come back; with 'one man, one vote,' political power has gone to the suburbs. Most decisions that affect the quality of people's lives are made in state capitals, if not in Washington itself. Few, if any, are made by the local people themselves anymore. Immense changes in values and life-styles spreading out from urban areas have alienated the generations from each other, among those who do remain in rural communities.

"The churches have been hard hit by all this change. Many people in those churches know they will have to develop new program and reach out to new people, but they are not skilled in change. In fact, many of them have very negative feelings about change—all change. That's understandable, because nearly every change they have experienced in the last several years has been bad for them.

"In our conference, we want to conduct an experiment, and we want you to be a part of that experiment. We want to go to a rural village congregation, together with you, and ask them if they would be willing to take some risks, in an attempt to discover how to initiate the kind of strong ministry which we believe is still possible in most rural village congregations."

So he said he saw potential in me and in rural congregations, especially together. He told me he knew I had skills in relating to people. He knew I wanted to live and minister in a rural community, even though I had made many mistakes in my ministry in my present parish. He said he thought I could learn from my mistakes. He believed I had been part of the problem, and I could be a part of the solution. He told me to look at all the rural congregations in our conference that had no pastor. He said

I could choose any one I wanted. He would go with me to visit that church's board and attempt to negotiate a contract that would include an experimental ministry.

The whole idea really excited me. It was a chance to start my ministry over, but on a new level. The conference staff would help me understand the particular parish I chose. I could be intentional and set goals. We could develop a plan, together with the local church board. We would work as a team toward the goals we set. We would all be in it together.

When I chose Stephentown and met with the church board, I found them surprisingly receptive to the whole idea. In addition to the usual responsibilities I would have as their pastor, we agreed to a three-year experimental ministry. During that time, we would make a concentrated effort to relate the congregation to different persons in the community. The board agreed that 25 percent of my ministry would be given over to this special effort. The conference promised some salary support, and also agreed to find outside resource persons to help develop needed program. Most important, we were to be accountable to each other. We agreed to meet together every three months in a steering committee, composed of me as the pastor, three representatives of the church board, and a representative of the conference. This steering committee would evaluate what had happened during the previous quarter, decide what changes, if any, we needed to make, and would set objectives for the next quarter.

The first thing I did when I began was to reflect on my past ministry. Was there anything I had done, especially in the early months of that ministry, that had led to my being so boxed in at the end of it? I didn't want to repeat the same mistakes in Stephentown.

As I reflected, I saw a number of important differences I should strive for, especially at the beginning of my ministry in this new congregation. In my former parish, I had tried to do too much too soon. I hadn't waited until I knew the people and, more importantly, until they knew me, before attempting to make any changes.

Second, I had brought to that parish ideas about things I thought should happen there, and then had tried to impose them.

Now I would take enough time to get to know people's needs and then let them suggest ways to meet them.

Third, I had failed to appreciate how costly change is to rural people. We mobile ministers forget what it means to be a permanent resident. When a new way of doing things doesn't work, or a new program backfires, we can move on to another parish and leave it all behind. But that permanent rural resident has to live with the results of change, usually for the rest of his life.

So I said I wanted no new programs for a while. I needed to get established.

My conference executive said, "Call us when you're ready."

As I said, I think those first few months are really critical. What you do while getting established can make or break you for the rest of your ministry in a church. This time I decided not to guess. I went to my board, and I asked them who could help me to get to know this congregation.

"Who really knows everybody?" I asked.

"George Simpson," they all agreed. "He's lived here all his life. He knows everybody, and everybody talks to him."

I went to see George Simpson. I said to him, "If you were in my shoes, trying to get established in this congregation, who would you go visit? Who are the important people to call on first?"

Not only did George Simpson tell me who to call on first, but when he got through telling me, he said, "I'm retired; I've got lots of time; I'll go with you. That way it will be easier for you to get to know these people."

For the next two months, two days every week, George Simpson and I went out and made calls. One by one, I got to know the opinion-makers in the congregation. They had a lot to say, so I did a lot of listening. In between the calls, George and I talked in the car. What the people we called on didn't tell me, George filled in. I kept a journal during those months; as a matter of fact, I still keep it. At night, I reflected about the people I had called on that day. Slowly, I began to feel with those people—to feel their hurts, their longings, and joys. I prayed for them. I began to appreciate them.

I began to understand how these rural people feel about the church. They don't come here for programs, at all. They come here for each other. For them, church is primarily a series of relationships they find meaningful. It's a place of caring and nurturing. It's more like a family than an association. They feel mutually responsible for one another. I could see that whatever program I might introduce would have to be shaped by this understanding of the church as a large family.

At the same time I was making those calls and getting acquainted with the congregation one by one, I was also meeting with various committees of the church, including the Christian Education Committee. They felt frustrated and guilty because of the dwindling Sunday school. At the same time, they really didn't believe that rebuilding it was possible. But they didn't know what else to do. One evening as we sat wondering, I shared with them my growing feeling that this congregation was one big family.

"When a family faces a crisis," I said, "often the best strategy is to bring the whole family together and decide together what to do."

That, in fact, is what we did. One Sunday morning at nine o'clock, we invited the whole congregation to breakfast. Would you believe that six dozen people came—old people, young people, parents and grandparents, children and teen-agers. After breakfast, members of the Christian Education Committee led discussion groups. They talked over such questions as, What do you think of our present Sunday school? What are its problems? Where should Christian nurture take place? What can we do to be effective in our Christian education?

In the discussion groups, we discovered that people were aware of the problems, but they had never been given the chance to air them, nor were they ever consulted for their suggestions. Now that the opportunity was given, the overwhelming consensus of the congregation was to attempt a new form of Christian education, directed at the whole family, rather than at just one member of it (the child). Moreover, people felt that an education program directed at the family, particularly one that would meet in homes, might provide a bridge to new people who were not active in any church. Church members felt that those people who found it difficult to come to a church building might, in time, feel more comfortable about taking that step if they came to know a few church members in their homes. So you see, the congregation was not only solving its own Christian education problem, it was attacking the problem of finding new members, as well.

I don't want to give the impression that establishing this new education program was easy. It wasn't. We decided to have family cluster Christian education in homes during the week. Eventually, we formed about eight of these family clusters. They met on various evenings of the week, roughly for two hours, beginning with supper. That turned out to be the best time period. People could really get to know each other during an informal meal together. The meeting was over soon enough for young children to go to bed and for people to attend other meetings that evening.

The format was clear enough, but we had neither curriculum nor trained leaders. I called the conference executive and asked for his promised help. It came in the form of a Christian education consultant, who met with leaders of the family clusters. He helped them develop needed leadership skills and also showed them how to develop their own curriculum. I discovered quickly the importance of the committed and capable support of a regional judicatory.

Most people are really surprised when I tell them we wrote our own curriculum in the family cluster groups. In fact, it was so good that eventually we published it and sold nearly a thousand copies. That experience taught me how seriously I had underestimated local church people. Amazing creativity and talent came forth in those family cluster groups. When we welcomed everyone's ideas, we discovered lots of people had ideas. When one cluster group developed a program, we wrote it up and shared it with the others.

As the church people in the family clusters became comfortable with one another and gained confidence, they began to invite their friends who were not church members to these week-night meetings. A surprising number of new people came. I know it sounds too simple, but we attracted new people because we aimed our program at new people, as well as at longstanding members. As a church, we showed we wanted to reach out, by doing it. We demonstrated that church, for us, is something more than what goes on in the church building on Sunday morning.

That openness has affected my whole ministry here. My agreement with the church board to spend 25 percent of my ministry outside the church has given me unusual freedom to relate to the community. Church members have never hesitated to recommend my availability to their unchurched friends, and I've felt free to accept commitments to work in the community. As a result, I have become, in many ways, the community's reconciler. I meet with several groups of students and teachers in the school, for example. I help them learn to practice good principles of communication. One result of this openness to the community is that there's always someone at my door. I get all kinds: people with marriage problems, people on drugs, people trying to cope with alcohol, or people who are just plain lonely. If you want to be looked upon as the community church—the church that relates to anybody and everybody—then you need to be willing and ready to deal with the different kinds of people who will come to you.

As a matter of fact, the program I've described is now gone. We don't have those family groups any more. But the effects have stayed. Understanding the church as being a series of relationships, as being there to reach out into the community— those basic attitudes have been repeated in program after program. We still have that open posture, that receptive attitude toward the community. That's what we stand for, and everybody knows it.

I don't want you to think the results came right away. It took us three or four years of investment before any new people joined the church, because it took that long for us to establish credibility as those people who genuinely care. Slowly the new people began to trust our intentions and gained confidence in our effectiveness. One by one, they began to invest their lives with us and to join. But I want to emphasize that it takes time to get results. If you don't realize that there will be a lag between the time you initiate the program and the time when people respond with a willingness to join the church, then you will be likely to terminate the program before it's had any permanent effect.

I looked at my watch. I had become so absorbed in his story that I would be very late for my next appointment. I thanked him for his time and willingness to share.

Then as I turned to go, I remembered, "One thing I have been wondering—what do you do about formal training in Christian education, especially for small children?"

"Oh," he laughed, "we're going to have a meeting about that tomorrow night. That's one problem we have never been able to solve. But one thing we have learned here is that we can't do everything well. After all, we are only a small church."

What We Can Learn from Stephentown

Most people hearing Jim Richards' story would conclude that the unusual achievements of the Stephentown congregation can be attributed largely to the fact that Richards is an exceptionally talented minister or that Stephentown is an unusually strong rural congregation or some combination of these circumstances. While there are some extraordinary dimensions to both this pastor's skills and the congregation's abilities, Stephentown is actually more *like* most rural congregations than it is different from them. Its revitalization occurred more because pastor and conference staff and local leaders found ways to work together so very effectively than because of its uniqueness. This combination unlocked some unusual resources in Stephentown. But similar resources are present, waiting to be released, in *most* small congregations. From the Stephentown experience, we can learn how to release those resources.

What have this pastor and church discovered and put into practice that enables them to be so effective?

First of all, they accept the constraints of ministry in a rural community and work positively within these constraints. Rural village congregations are rural. By this, I mean that they are not urban, and especially, they are not suburban. Surburban- or urban-trained pastors and church planners and judicatories think of the church in terms of "programs." *Rural people think of the church in terms of relationships.* Relationships are supremely important, because the rural community is so stable, and because everyone is so exposed and identifiable. With few exceptions, rural people deal with the same faces day by day and year after year. Even those who move into a rural community tend to stay there.

Rural people view the church through their relationships and experience it in terms of their relationships. Jim Richards shapes his ministry in Stephentown to recognize the primacy of relationships. He knows that any new program he introduces is examined not so much in terms of what it is in itself, but according to its effect on established relationships. He realized that *any* suggested basic change in mode of living will be painfully considered, because the person being asked to change knows he will have to live with the implications of any change for the rest of his life.

Second, Jim Richards' entry into the congregation was well planned and appropriate to the context. He took great pains to build a solid relationship of trust, not only with the official program leaders—persons who held formal power in the congregation—but also with the so-called opinion-makers—those who wield large influence through the informal power structure of the congregation. When he did call people together to make program decisions, they all felt they knew him and could trust him, because one by one, they had come to know him personally beforehand, in the safety and privacy of their own homes.

Third, Jim Richards is well suited and personally committed to this place and type of ministry. He comes to Stephentown as a mature person who knows who he is and what he can do, with realistic expectations of himself and the congregation. He has personal assets which equip him well for a rural ministry. He is quiet, undramatic, not at all imposing, always more ready to listen than to talk.

As one person observed, "When you're around Jim, somehow he helps you do your own thing."

In a ministry where relationships predominate as they do in the small, rural church, personal characteristics are often much more important to the success of the ministry than is the ability to develop and execute effective programs. The pastor's Christian commitment is also indispensable. In the close scrutiny that comes through ongoing, face-to-face relationships, people will discover a pastor's basic character. Church members often explain the effectiveness of Jim Richard's ministry by saying simply that he is a Christian and genuinely cares about people.

All this is not to say that Jim Richards lacks talent or competence. It is to say that his talent and competence lie largely in his ability to relate to people, and in his realistic understanding of people. He sees people as a mixture of good and bad, and not always the same from moment to moment. He does not see people as threats; therefore he does not need to dominate them or control them; he is able to relate to them openly and to enhance them. He has developed the capacity to learn from his own experience and from his own mistakes, and as a result, is free to help other people learn from their own experience and their mistakes.

Fourth, conference leaders were able to see potential in Jim Richards and to help him realize that potential, even though he was an apparent failure in his first parish. They were able to discern what he could become and invited him into a ministry where his potential could be realized. They stayed with him, lending support as he began his ministry. They gave him the freedom he needed, but were present with resources when he asked for help.

Fifth, Jim Richards entered Stephentown as a secure pastor who could accept outside resources and consultants, who knew how to direct this help to those points where it would be most effective, and who was not threatened by it. Insecure pastors generally do not seek outside help, because the effectiveness of others threatens them; or, if they do seek it, they tend to discount its effectiveness for their congregations.

It can be said, to the credit of the outside resourcers at Stephentown, that they knew how to provide help without threatening either the pastor or the local lay leaders. Astute resourcers such as those in Stephentown *never* intrude between the pastor and the lay leaders, or between either and the congregation. They always enhance the effectiveness of the local leaders by strengthening their effectiveness with the local group, never by showing them up.

Sixth, the vision of the pastor and the church board in Stephentown is not limited to their own congregation, but includes the entire community. This breadth of vision not only widens the possibilities of Jim Richards' ministry, but eventually benefits the church with additional members. His activity in the community builds bridges to the church, across which strangers can travel to become part of the church. He works with various community groups. He carries on an active counseling ministry with students and teachers in the public school. When people in the community discover he is competent, as they work with him in community groups, many of them transfer that confidence to the church. His competence, commitment, and humanity, acted out in his activity in the community, make him believable as a spiritual leader, in the eyes of those outside the church.

The church board's willingness to open church facilities to nonchurch groups also is a positive factor attracting new persons into eventual church membership. The church plays host regularly to such groups as Parents Without Partners and Alcoholics Anonymous, and is in the process of beginning a food co-op. Jim Richards believes that opening the church building to outsiders helps build important bridges to the community.

"Somewhere along the line, there's going to be somebody who is a parent without a partner, or who has a friend who is one, or they have someone in AA or Al-Anon. People who have no connection with the church to begin with are constantly coming onto the grounds. They see me around. I'm in the groups, doing what I can. They see the church as willing to donate the building, and they see church members donating their time. All that makes an impact on these people. They come to see the church as being for them."

Seventh, Jim Richards' ministry was effective because it was based on a mutual understanding of what the major thrusts of that ministry would be, before it began. The open negotiation between him and the church board, facilitated by the conference staff, specifically

25

for purposes of defining the experimental dimension of his ministry, actually had the unanticipated benefit of facilitating a clear and open agreement about the nature of the entire ministry. He and the church board began with the same expectations. This congruence of purpose enabled them to work together effectively as a team from the beginning. They wasted little or no energy struggling over differences.

A second set of learnings grew out of the surprisingly dynamic family cluster program that was developed in Stephentown.

This ordinary congregation in an ordinary village developed a highly innovative program that attracted a large number of new and different participants to the congregation. A seminary student, who spent his summer assignment with the Stephentown congregation, conducted a survey of the family groups. Comparing the data he gathered from the groups with the congregation as a whole, he shows highly significant differences. While 43 percent of the members of the church at that time were male, 56 percent of the participants in the family groups were male. While 18 percent of the church membership was twenty to thirty-four years of age, 35 percent of the family group participants were in that age group. While 43 percent of the family group participants were college graduates, only 16 percent of the church participants were.

The qualitative results of this program are equally as impressive as the statistical. Family groups built lasting primary relationships which involved much more than the church. Participants formed deep and lasting friendships. Church became an experience close to life. It moved out of the building. It became accessible to outsiders. The clusters brought entire families into the church. The congregation's character as a family church was firmly established in the community.

The success of this experimental program has had another important lasting effect. Some present church leaders continue to think of the process of innovation as safe. Several persons who came into the church through the family group program have been elected by the congregation to the church board.

Their willingness to try new and different programs, rooted in their positive experience with the experimental program of the family cluster makes them extremely valuable board members.

Finally, the family clusters uncovered an unforeseen reservoir of local talent. With the conference consultant acting as a catalyst, local leaders were able to develop their own curriculum and write and produce their own materials.

What can we learn from this successful program about the *process* of innovation? What made possible so much change in this church? What were the key factors?

The first factor fundamental to the successful development of this program was the manner in which the program was introduced. Any leader wishing to suggest change in a small rural church will need to demonstrate first that he understands (feels) the situation in which people find themselves, and that he is sufficiently loyal and devoted to warrant their taking a risk. Little or no program change is likely to be accepted in a rural congregation until this trust relationship is earned. Pastor Richards demonstrated that he was sensitive to the natural inclinations, as well as the needs, in Stephentown. The need for Christian nurture was quickly apparent. The natural inclination to meet that need through the family nurture program emerged much more slowly and subtly. Jim Richards took time to help the congregation gain a common viewpoint and find a structure or means to implement the program that would be suitable for *them*.

Second, sufficient resources were available to establish the program solidly. Once the need for program development became clear, Jim Richards could turn to the judicatory and find sufficient help. Equally as important as the specific program resourcing was the judicatory's financial support to the congregation. A guarantee of adequate financial support took economic pressure off the congregation. This gave them breathing space. It freed resources, which would have been consumed in a fight for survival, to be applied to program development and innovation.

Stephentown's experience contains a clear challenge to those judicatories that tend to give a *little* aid to *most* of their struggling congregations. We could term this a "buckshot" policy. Its actual effect may be to keep most congregations at a struggling level. If we assume the pattern at Stephentown to be an alternative that could be appled generally, then focusing a *significant* amount of resourcing on a *few* congregations long enough to enable them to become solidly established, would be likely to prove, in time, a much more effective policy. Judicatories could not help all their congregations at once, but those they did help would become viable and able to survive on their own. Once they did, the judicatory could move on to others and, eventually, most congregations would be substantially strengthened.

Third, the ongoing partnership of the judicatory, the pastor, and the church was also a significant factor in the process of innovation. Pastor and congregation became accustomed to turning to others for help. Looking beyond the local congregation for suggestions and direction became a natural experience. Such an attitude is indispensable in our time. Few, if any, congregations or pastors have sufficient resources of innovative ability to meet the needs of a congregation adequately. Such needs can be met only through cooperative efforts.

Fourth, the outside resourcing the congregation received was clearly effective. Suitable curriculum for local needs, for example, was not available. The Christian education consultant was able to relate helpfully to that problem. He worked wih local leaders to look at their specific needs and then helped them to develop program and materials to relate to those needs. He worked through them, and he enhanced their role and effectiveness. He directed attention to them, and they became more solidly established.

Fifth, accountability to someone beyond the local level was another important factor in establishing the innovative program at Stephentown. The fact that there was someone coming back periodically to ask how it was going and what the leaders had been doing was an important fact all by itself. Each upcoming planning session encouraged leaders to fulfill the commitments they had made during the previous planning session.

Sixth, the fact that someone beyond the church itself noticed them and invested in them made the congregation feel important and confident about the quality of its life and its program. In Pastor Richards' words, "If you say, 'Here's something we want you to do; it's an experiment, and you have to provide the resources and the structure in which it can take place. But we'll invest our resources in your ability to come through with something,' I think that attitude gave the congregation confidence and support. It made them feel good about themselves and also opened the possibilities of really becoming very creative."

Outside attention also made Jim Richards conscious of his own leadership style. It encouraged him to ask what kind of leader he was, whether what he was doing was effective and whether it was getting results. It encouraged him to seek continuing education.

Ministers and congregations often stagnate because no one notices them and challenges them. If someone did, they would probably rise to the challenge. Saying, "We believe in you and would like to do something significant where you are; we think you are special," would encourage many ministers to make the kinds of changes and to seek the kind of developments that Jim Richards did in Stephentown.

Seventh, the willingness of both the pastor and the congregation to risk was undoubtedly another key factor contributing to this congregation's ability to innovate. Perhaps the presence of conference staff and the guarantee of conference support initially encouraged congregation and pastor to take risks. But I cannot help feeling that many pastors and congregations could take more risks profitably than most of them do. Arthur Tennies, a researcher who studied the experimental ministry at Stephentown, wrote in his report,

> The best way to find out whether family groups or any other program will work is to try it. This runs up against the idea that failure is intolerable—and this is nonsense. The world isn't going to collapse because a pastor tried something and it didn't work. We are too uptight most of the time in the church. The pastor tries something new in worship, and it fails. So what? Why should people walk out in a huff? If he insists on failing with it ten times, that would be different. Pastors and congregations should try

29

things with the idea that some won't work. A good batter still makes an out seven out of ten times.

Eighth, Stephentown's success is tied to perseverance. Two important principles are almost always at work in the process of innovation. The first I call the lag effect, and the second I call the snowballing effect. In the research community, the lag effect is also called the half-life. This can be defined as the amount of time one needs to invest in any new program before there are any apparent results. In Stephentown, there were no apparent results, as far as the *church* was concerned, for at least three years. While the family groups attracted new people and there were new participants, the new people did not become church members or begin to support the church financially in any significant numbers until the fourth and fifth years. Indeed, the fourth and fifth years, when the conference funds were no longer coming to the congregation, were years of real struggle. For a while, the pastor took a parttime job to support himself, but he and the congregation continued to persevere in the new directions the ministry had taken. By the sixth year, and especially in the seventh year, the newer members had generated enough economic support to make the congregation economically self-sufficient.

The importance of perseverance and recognition of the lag effect is obvious. If pastor and congregation had insisted upon results in the early years and had given up the program direction when results did not come, the entire project would probably have been written off as a failure. Looking back, we can see how fundamental to the success of this project were the basic ingredients that went into it. The fact that pastor and congregation had similar goals and expectations saved them from blaming each other when results weren't achieved as quickly as they had anticipated. The fact that the innovative program was solidly related to the life-style of the community reduced the likelihood that the congregation would discard it as a novelty or inappropriate when results were slow in coming. The guarantee of judicatory support and the repeated presence of outside consultants gave local leaders frequent opportunities to check their perceptions and receive needed encouragement.

The snowballing effect is intertwined with the lag effect. It refers to the fact that most new programs are slow to attract interest in the beginning. The more people they attract, the more they gain the capacity to attract, as they move along. In the first months and years of the new ministry at Stephentown, only a few outsiders would risk participation. But the longer the program rolled on, the more it attracted new people, and the more new people it attracted, the more it gained capacity to attract new people. The church established a new reputation in the community as a family church and as a place where people could find ministry of exceptionally high quality.

The snowballing effect means that any new direction of ministry or innovative program, once the novelty stage is past, will develop very slowly for some time. As it becomes established, it gains greater and greater momentum and capacity to attract. If leaders do not persevere through the meager results of the early months, they lose the possibility of success in the later years.

The story of Stephentown illustrates the remarkable possibilities that lurk in many small congregations caught in declining communities. There were some unusual factors to be sure, that helped this congregation realize its hidden potential. Jim Richards has some unusual talents, and the conference brought a significant amount of resources into the project. But most of the successful growth of this congregation cannot be attributed to the unusual ingredients. Most small congregations and most small church pastors could practice the principles that were fundamental in fostering the dramatic developments in Stephentown.

In summary, these principles are:

1. A pastor will be much more effective in a church and community in harmony with his own personal attributes and commitments.

2. A pastor increases the possibilities for an effective ministry when he addresses the *unique* needs and potentials of his congregation and community.

3. Beginnings are crucial. A well-planned and well-executed beginning is almost indispensable to an effective ministry.

4. A church that includes its entire community within the focus of its programming and its pastor's responsibilities raises its own possibilities immensely.

5. Outside resourcers, especially those designing and establishing new programs, can be of immense help to local leaders.

6. Regular external accountability encourages local leaders to fulfill their commitments. It helps to insure that plans will be carried out.

7. Being in the limelight can encourage a congregation to improve its performance.

8. It takes a great deal of perseverance to establish an innovative program solidly.

II. How to Succeed or Fail by Merging

Introduction

Merger is the most difficult of all church organizational adjustments. The two case histories and the analysis which follows present contrasting mergers: one highly successful (East Park), and the other (Winchester) hardly successful at all. When we place these two experiences side by side, we are able to see clearly the key elements that need to be present for an effective merger.

The Cases

Winchester

George Carpenter was a survivor. That's the only way anybody made it in Jersey City.

He never tired of repeating his motto, "Do what you have to do first; explain later."

Fresh from seminary, he came to serve the dual charge of Winchester, a small village church on a hill, just barely on the edge of a large metropolitan area, and West Winchester, a very small congregation located down at the crossroads, two miles further out. About the only thing those two churches ever had in common was their pastor. The distance between the village and the crossroads cluster of houses is still commonly referred to as the "longest two miles in the world."

At the top of the hill, in freshly painted, stately homes, live the Adams, the Bensons, and the Holmes. These families furnish the area's lawyers, businessmen, and town doctor. At the bottom of the hill, in houses scattered along the river, around what used to be the tannery, live the Bashwingers, the Hertzogs, and the Rivenbergs. "Skip" Bashwinger runs the auto graveyard; Bill Hertzog is reputed to be the best welder in three counties; Sam Rivenberg's trucks will move anything that he and his brothers can carry, which means just about everything.

The church at the top of the hill is set in the midst of a large village green—its tall steeple topped by a majestic weather vane.

The governing board of the little church next to the tannery had talked for years about the importance of painting their building. But most of those who had painted the church in the past were now too old to climb ladders, and the young people just seemed to be too busy. Nor were church members able to raise enough money to hire the job done.

It didn't take very long for George Carpenter to decide what he had to do. Within three weeks, he was convinced of the foolishness of holding one service for nearly a hundred people in the village and another, attended by a faithful two dozen, only two miles away. Those two miles just didn't seem to be very long to George Carpenter.

"We need to be efficient," he told the board in the church at the top of the hill. "We've got too much property between these two congregations. Besides, I can't give proper attention to Christian education if every Sunday morning at nine-thirty I've got to lead the worship service at the other church; and I'm getting exhausted with all the meetings that it takes to run two organizations. I think we ought to get everyone together and have one church."

That solution made sense to many, though not all, of the lawyers and the businessmen. It was certainly sound from an economic point of view. Even from a program point of view, they felt the village church could provide a good deal for the people at the bottom of the hill.

So they said to George Carpenter, "Go ahead and see what you can do."

That was all the encouragement George needed. He wrote an elaborate proposal, detailing arguments in favor of the merger and spelling out the way he felt the merger would benefit both congregations. He placed the proposal before the board of the church at the bottom of the hill. He explained various items in the proposal carefully. The new church would have a board composed proportionately of people from the two churches. The proposal guaranteed worship services and Sunday school at both buildings for two years. It included a number of scheduled events that would give the people from the two congregations an opportunity to get to know one another and to work together. At the end of two years, the joint board would decide what to do about the property, whether to continue worship services and church school at both locations the year round, and work out other details of the merger.

George's logic overwhelmed them, especially when he showed them what good stewardship it would be to have one congregation and one set of buildings, in place of two. When he called for discussion, no one could find a voice. He took the silence as agreement. They approved the proposal, as did the board at the church at the top of the hill. Implementing the plan called for a joint meeting of the two congregations to be held a month hence. At considerable expense, the entire ten-page document was sent to every family in both congregations.

When the evening of the joint meeting came, there were fewer people in attendance than George had expected; but there were enough for a technical quorum. So George went ahead, especially after he was encouraged in a conversation with a local government official, who said that probably a lot of people were not present because they didn't much care which way the vote went. After very little discussion, the proposal passed with only three dissenting votes.

So the two congregations—Winchester and West Winchester—became almost, but not quite, one. It was a marriage of convenience and, unfortunately, like most marriages of convenience, serious problems soon became apparent.

The two years of continued services in both churches went by slowly for George, but very quickly for those at the church down by the river. For reasons not apparent to anyone, attendance dwindled; the thirty regular worshipers dropped to twenty. When the joint board met to decide the matter of worship services in the future, a bitter debate broke out when someone moved to terminate services at the little church. In fact, the debate grew so bitter that the board decided to postpone any decision about the worship services and the property for another year. They hoped that would give an opportunity "for things to die down."

Actually, the opposite occurred. During the next year, discontent growing out of the merger increased. Pastor and board were bombarded with questions: Had there been adequate notice of the merger? Why had no one explained what the merger would mean? What would become of the buildings if the board decided to sell them? Under a barrage of criticism, three members of the joint board, who came originally from the church by the river, and who had voted in favor of the merger, resigned. The board made a serious effort to find other persons who had come from the small church to replace them. It failed.

Pressure on George increased. People began to complain that his sermons were not down-to-earth. "How could a city boy understand country people?" they asked. There were other criticisms. People along the river said he was spending all his time with people in the village. People in the village said he was spending all his time with the people along the river. Everyone complained he was spending too much time in denominational activities. When an attractive opportunity came his way, it didn't take him long to decide to accept it. He has survived, but not in Winchester. The merged congregation he left behind, now less than one-half the size of the combined churches that produced it, continues a precarious existence.

East Park

She was seventy-six years of age. She had spent her whole life in East Park. She gave the second stained-glass window on the right wall of the United Methodist church sanctuary as a memorial to her parents thirty years ago, when the building was last refurbished. And she was crying.

"Oh, Pastor Tod," she sobbed, "I don't think I can bear to leave this old building." Her breakdown had come unexpectedly in the middle of a planning committee meeting. That they had to do something was apparent to them all. Nearly one hundred bricks had broken away from the northwest wall of the church building and fallen to the sidewalk, two nights before. Miraculously, no one was hurt.

"I know all the practical reasons we can't go on," Mary Evans continued through her tears, "but I'm frightened. I don't know whether I will be able to pray in another building!"

The minister's heart reeled. The paper full of facts and figures he had been presenting in the meeting, sound as it was, suddenly seemed very unimportant. He recalled his own struggles to learn to pray. How important certain things had become to him: the Bible his father had given him; the old chair in which he always had his morning devotions. He knew they helped him to pray. He understood how costly leaving this building would be to Mary Evans, who had prayed in the same pew for three quarters of a century.

"It's nearly nine-thirty," he said to the committee. "Let's call it a night." They all agreed.

It was after eleven o'clock when he finally drove Mary Evans the two blocks to her apartment. As he helped her up the steps, she suddenly straightened up, turned to him, and said, "I can go along with the change, if we have to do it. I wouldn't want to bind another generation to pray in a building they will soon have to leave." Tod knew he had stayed with her long enough to help her find resources within herself to face the inevitable. Many times before during these past three years, he had spent hours similar to those he invested on this night with Mary Evans.

Tod Maclean had come into the pastorate of the Second Avenue Presbyterian Church with complete awareness of the dilemmas he would face. There were one hundred ten active members—eighty-six of them over fifty, and sixty-four of those over sixty-five. Only a few members still drove in from the suburbs. Most participants came from the two-family houses and apartments in the neighborhood immediately surrounding the church building. The church and the neighborhood had been losing ground for at least thirty years. The Methodist church down the block, where Mary Evans belonged, had the same problems as the Presbyterian church. In fact, they were worse, because the congregation was smaller. Both churches were happy when Tod agreed to act as supply pastor to the Methodist church, in return for one-third of his support. Tod knew he would have, at the most, five years to survive in the arrangement. He had looked at the trends, both for the churches and the neighborhood; he knew where they were headed. He might slow them down, but he could not stop them.

Tod read everything he could find about the survival of small city churches with shrinking resources in changing neighborhoods. He quickly surveyed the resources available to his two congregations. He visited the city hall, especially the urban-planning agencies. He talked to the social agency people who worked in his neighborhood. He consulted staff from both denominations. Tod knew that if he was going to help these congregations, he would need all the expert insight and help he could get.

But most important, Tod talked with church members like Mary Evans, one by one. He shared honestly with them the difficult decisions he saw ahead. He listened with genuine concern to their reactions. He talked with them until he was sure they knew that he understood how they felt.

In his preaching, Tod encouraged both congregations to have faith and vision. He did his best to make worship a genuinely helpful experience. During three years of calling and preaching and caring, most of the members of the two congregations grew to love and trust him. He was so open that even those few who didn't particularly like him at least came to respect him.

But, in time, the unavoidable decisions had to be made. The two congregations would need to decide which, if either, building they would sell, before a date set by Urban Renewal. After that date, the agency would no longer purchase any additional property. A large joint committee of the two congregations was formed to explore options for the churches. The committee spent its first year probing feelings and gaining the confidence of the two congregations. After exploring various alternatives, the committee decided to look seriously at the possibility of merger.

There were many problems to face; the committee divided into smaller groups and allocated specific tasks to each. Both churches had endowments. How could and should they be used? The endowment subcommittee retained an attorney to advise them. They also visited with relatives of all those who had left money to the churches to discover their wishes and follow them wherever possible. Another subcommittee attacked the difficult problem of which building should be sold. They employed an architect. His report indicated that the Methodist church had serious structural problems that would take many thousands of dollars to rectify. The Presbyterian church, on the other hand, was not only smaller, but structurally sound. Moreover, the money gained from the sale of one church property would help defray the costs of maintaining the building that was retained.

Another group explored the matter of denominational affiliation. Was it possible, or even advisable, to have a union congregation belonging to both denominations? They decided that to do so would encourage divided loyalties and recommended that the merged congregation affiliate with the United Methodist denomination, especially since it was the Presbyterian building that was being retained. In terms of individual membership, they recommended that all present church members be given automatic membership in both denominations, but that new members become members only of the United Methodist church.

Another group explored the matter of benevolence funds. They decided to recommend that those funds raised through endowment income go to the denomination in which the person giving the endowment had held membership. All other benevolence funds would go to the denomination with which the congregation ultimately affiliated. The negotiations these

39

subcommittees carried on were often difficult, but Tod encouraged them to face each area openly, directly, and thoroughly.

At the end of several months, a plan of union was prepared. It dealt with all dimensions of the congregation's life. It included specific and detailed proposals for each area, indicating exactly what the committee was proposing, and why. Over the next three months, either a member of the committee or the pastor visited with each church member to explain the plan of union. Several members made helpful suggestions that were incorporated into the plan. During December, the plan was presented to each congregation individually. It passed overwhelmingly. Later that winter, it was presented to each denomination and was approved. The plan became effective at a service of celebration on Pentecost, the following year. The service began with a procession in which members of the old Methodist church carried their pulpit Bible, communion ware, flags, and paraments through the streets of the city to the former Presbyterian church building, testifying publicly to the entire community that these two congregations had, in fact, become one. Every year on Pentecost, the congregation celebrates the birthday of their church.

Three years after the merger was consummated, Mary Evans died, strong in the faith, leaving her picture of the stained-glass window that used to be on the right wall of the old Methodist church to Pastor Tod. She knew he would understand why. He did.

What We Can Learn from Winchester and East Park

The central questions that arise when we read the story of these two mergers are What made the difference? Why was one merger so successful and the other such a disaster?

We can identify a number of reasons. Some have to do with differences in the context in which the two mergers occurred. Others have to do with the leadership skills of the pastors. Still others have to do with the process the congregation followed in consummating the merger.

Let us look first at differences in the social contexts. The two

East Park churches were located in the same social context. By contrast, there were so many radical differences between the communities of Winchester and West Winchester, that this merger would probably have failed under the leadership of a highly skilled pastor, even if the congregations had followed the best processes of organizational development.

When two congregations are based in radically different social contexts, a successful merger between them is highly unlikely. While church is much more than a social experience in their lives, most people's style of church participation is deeply shaped by their own particular social experience. They are attracted to a church made up of people similar to them socially, with a program that relates to their interests and concerns, and a leader who speaks to their needs, who often has a life-style similar to theirs.

Drastic social differences between the predominant groups in Winchester and West Winchester almost preclude forming a single congregation that can speak to the needs and expectations of both groups. The moderately affluent professionals who compose the bulk of the congregation in Winchester represent a group who are successful, articulate, well-educated, and accustomed to assuming leadership responsibility and giving directions. They have above-average resources to face the challenges of social change; they expect to rise above these challenges. In other words, they expect to go through the process of change and emerge as winners on the other side.

On the other hand, the people at the bottom of the hill, in the little church next to the tannery, with much less formal education, are not so articulate. Their experiences of change have been largely experiences of loss. Most of them do not have the ability to advocate for themselves to protect their own interests. They are accustomed to taking direction—to adapting, rather than determining. When faced with change they tend to withdraw.

Moreover, there is history of antagonism between the crossroads and the village that stretches back a hundred years. Crossroad people believe village people have taken advantage of them at many points throughout that history. One resident told me the township had not been able to pass a school budget for ten years. He said the process of school centralization, symbolized by the loss of the one-room school, appears to the crossroads people to be one more example of a continuing loss of control over their own lives. The decision to locate the new central school near the village, and the domination of the school board, especially the school administration, by village-type people, represents another instance where village people control the change, and crossroads people have to adapt.

The East Park congregations were as socially similar as the Winchester congregations were different. The two churches in East Park were located only a block apart and served nearly identical constituencies. Most members had shared common experiences for the last thirty or forty years, many of them for more than half a century. Most of them still lived in the neighborhood around the church buildings. They had a common high investment in what became of that neighborhood and the institutions that served that neighborhood. They were similar in age and social group. They tended to have about the same educational level, and worked in similar jobs. Thus, when they came together to face their institutional church problems, they shared a common experience, a common life-style, a common vocabulary, common needs, and common concerns. With the help of skilled leadership, they were able to surmount difficult obstacles to develop common goals, and eventually to adopt merger as a common strategy to meet those goals.

Turning now to a second factor which contributes to the development of a successful merger: *The formal organizational process which the East Park churches employed to develop their merger was very well designed and executed.* We can identify several important differences between the processes followed in East Park, as opposed to those followed in Winchester. Leaders in East Park exposed the thorny issues. They defined them. They met them head on. They resolved them. As a result, there were no leftovers to trouble the new congregation.

In Winchester, by contrast, leaders attempted to avoid many serious issues. They postponed facing them until after the merger, in the mistaken belief that it would be easier to face them then. They circumvented the question of which building would ultimately be retained, for example, as well as the length of time worship services would be held at both sites. These and other issues the congregations did not face in the period of negotiation prior to the merger were much more difficult to resolve after the merger, when many months of uncertainty had led to a high level of anxiety. Differences over these unresolved issues added more fuel to the existing animosity between the two congregations and communities. Procrastination made matters much worse than if the congregations had confronted their real differences prior to the merger.

Similar differences might have led to equally serious ruptures in East Park. For example, members of each church had strong attachments to their respective buildings. There was also the matter of which denomination they should affiliate with, or whether to affiliate with both. Each church had endowments.

However, the East Park churches drew a large number of persons together to face each issue squarely. They gathered the facts in full view of everyone. They defined, publicized, and explored *various* options. They searched for a consensus around which all elements within the two congregations could gather. At times, differences were difficult to negotiate; but they were negotiated. Leaders took their time. As a result, church members entered the merger knowing that the major issues were resolved. They saw the future as clearly as it was possible to see it. There were very few leftover uncertainties to wonder about. They were free to move ahead and to go about the business of becoming a new congregation.

The major role that lay leaders played in East Park probably accounts for much of the greater organizational effectiveness there. Tod encouraged them to take major continuing responsibility in the merger process. He knew the lay leaders would be much more likely to acknowledge the results of the process and to work hard to establish the new church, if they had an important role in shaping it.

In Winchester and West Winchester, by contrast, George Carpenter dominated the entire merger process. Lay leaders played a very minor role. As a result, now that this merger has not worked out as well as promised, the lay leaders feel trapped in a church they had only a small role in shaping. When criticism and pressure mount, they tend to disavow responsibility. They believe themselves to be in an impossible situation, and probably they are right. The old hurts continue to be so fundamental in Winchester, and so widespread throughout the congregation, that they still frustrate efforts to move ahead. Given the atmosphere of tension, many who might participate still stay away. The current leaders experience continuing difficulty in enlisting support.

A third factor that explains the contrasting experiences of these two mergers is the effective employment of outside resourcers at key points in one case, and the lack of their use in the other. Data needed to make controversial decisions are much less suspect if they come from independent, clearly unbiased sources. Thus, the question of which building to retain in East Park was easier to resolve, when data was presented by an independent engineering firm. The only data the Winchester churches had when facing a similar question came from church members. While that data may have provided an accurate assessment of the feasibility of using various buildings, it all emerged from insiders. It was very difficult to disassociate what a person said was true, from what his associations would lead people to believe he wanted.

Then there is the additional matter of competence. An opinion offered by an engineering firm is much more likely to be competent than one offered by amateurs. Though members may not want to do what the engineering firm suggests, they at least can find some comfort in the fact that the firm's suggestion is probably sound. Thus, they are less likely to feel they have lost, even when they do not get what they want.

A fourth important difference that emerges when we study these two mergers is in the area of communication: Formal institution-to-members communication was excellent in East Park, but very poor in Winchester. In Winchester, only the church boards received information in a form and at a rate that enabled them to stay in touch with the merger process. While it is true that all church members had the merger proposal some weeks before it was formally acted upon, receiving the information in a lengthy and complicated proposal was not helpful to most of them. This was especially true for members of the small church along the river, where, as we have already noted, most residents had little formal education and were not skilled speakers. They really did not foresee the impact the merger would have in their lives. No one sat down with them to explain it. Even those who did attend the large group meetings felt embarrassed by their inability to understand all the information. They were hesitant to speak out or ask questions in a large gathering.

In East Park, by contrast, pastor and board members visited with nearly all church members individually to talk over the merger before *any* written documents were circulated. Members received frequent communication about various aspects of the merger proposal, such as buildings to be utilized, endowments, denominational affiliation, and so on, as each was being developed. Throughout the months of negotiation, there were frequent opportunities for interchange of opinion and information, both in home visits and in small group meetings. Being on one of several working committees gave a large percentage of the membership firsthand knowledge of the difficult problems the church faced. Communications sent to members presented *various* options, and they were encouraged and provided with the means to make comments and suggestions. As a result of this thorough sharing process, extending through many months, when the time to vote on the proposal arrived, most members of both churches understood very well what they were voting for. In Winchester, quite the opposite was true. Few church members understood clearly what they had voted for, even after they had voted.

When the process of organizational change excludes most people from meaningful participation, they have few, if any, opportunities to test their understanding of what the change will mean. Different people will draw different conclusions. When the result turns out not to be what they expected, they often feel they have been deceived. In Winchester, that sense of deception led to the angry withdrawal of church members, and even board members, in the months following the merger. Even now, some years afterward, many of those who withdrew still carry with them these feelings of betrayal and are not willing to participate in the merged congregation.

An effective communications system within a congregation is three-way: down, around, and up. It provides members with information they need, in a form they can utilize to participate effectively (down). It offers opportunities and resources for members to share, test, and assimilate information through interaction (around). It provides ample channels for feedback, through which members have access to those in authority and the ability to exert effective influence in the decision-making process (up).

Closely related to communication is a fifth factor contributing to the success of the East Park merger: During the months of negotiation, pastor and lay leaders gave careful individual attention to all persons, especially weaker and nonleader types. Tod's appreciation of what this merger would cost individuals like Mary Evans, and his unwillingness to trample on their feelings to effect a quick organizational change were fundamental to the ultimate success of the East Park merger. His caring ministry to the hurts and fears of countless church members in both congregations was his most important role throughout the months of preparation.

To organizationally oriented people, merger seems the logical option to follow when short resources make the continued survival of two separate institutions impossible. To Mary Evans (and others like her who make up the *majority* of most congregations), merger means the loss of her pew and the stained-glass window she gave to assuage the pain of a deep personal loss. Unless someone like Tod helps her to accept yet another loss, she is not free to go into the new era, which can begin with the transition to a new congregation. Even those persons who do not have as deep a personal investment as Mary Evans will be likely to experience a sense of failure in the months during the movement toward a merger. No explanation of what is to be gained can eradicate their feelings of failure—the church they have struggled to keep alive for years, even generations, is now going to die. Someone needs to help them mourn, or they will not be free to get on with the business of living. They deeply need pastoral care. When they receive it, as they did in East

Park, they are able to move through their feelings of loss and guilt. When they do not, they become permanently mired and simply cannot move on to make a transition.

The ultimate tragedy, of course, is that once the merger occurs those left behind truly have no place. The congregation in which they once had a place is gone. The new congregation is not theirs, because they did not invest themselves in shaping it. At first glance, it appears they withdraw because they are angry. Actually, many of them stay away because they suffer from unresolved grief and are unable to find a place in what they feel is an alien congregation.

The lack of access experienced by those not considered in a merger process can be painfully obvious. The building the church board decided to keep open in Winchester has a long flight of stairs. The building abandoned in West Winchester could be entered at ground level. The majority of members at West Winchester are old; many cannot climb stairs, or climb only with great difficulty. The fact that the board of the merged church in Winchester voted in favor of the church with the long flight of stairs, without realizing how formidable this would be to older members, demonstrates how out of touch pastor and board there were with the needs of nonleaders.

Sixth, the process leading up to the merger in East Park opened the way for integration following the merger; in Winchester, the process leading up to the merger made integration after the merger extremely difficult.

The merged church never turns out to be exactly what people expect it to be. As one church member put it, "The experience of merger turns out to be quite different from what people thought it would be. So they end up feeling they have been 'had,' or that someone didn't explain to them adequately what merger would mean. In fairness to the leadership, I think we have to say that even the leaders, who have greater opportunity to consider the options, often do not themselves know what merger will really mean. Thus, even when no one intends to deceive, people can end up feeling they were deceived—that they bought a pig in a poke, and they are not happy with the pig they got."

This element of the unpredictable, inherent in all organizational change, demonstrates again why establishing and maintaining sound relationships is so indispensable to the success of a merger. When formal structures give way, healthy, informal structures and relationships become all the more important. They provide a bridge from the old organization to the new, in a period when there is no familiar organization to depend on. When relationships are not healthy and open during this transition period, the resulting tension and strain may actually cause the new organization to break apart. This early fragmenting happened in Winchester. So many members dropped away in the years immediately following the merger that the congregation existing today is much smaller in size than either congregation that composed it.

In East Park, pastor and lay leaders did not challenge the existing support structures of the old churches until they were certain that relationships were sound enough to carry members during the time of transition. Then they worked through these open relationships to integrate the two congregations into one—to forge a new, single, organizational identity. They brought as many persons as possible into the forging of that singular identity, not only informally, but also formally, through such symbolic events as the Pentecost procession, testifying publicly that these two churches were now to be one. In the months following the merger, while the organization was as yet untried, people could cope with unexpected disappointments or surprises, because of the relationships of trust with one another, their lay leaders, and Pastor Tod.

Someone once remarked: "The most important function of leadership is to restate the vision." The constant restating of the positive vision of the future by Tod and the church's lay leaders, especially in bleaker moments at East Park, was critical. Such positive reminders made it all seem worthwhile. *This element of vision, so clearly present in East Park, and almost completely lacking in Winchester, is the seventh major difference between these two mergers.*

These notes, taken by the secretary at a committee meeting in East Park, are very revealing.

The third General Committee meeting of the Second Avenue United Presbyterian and the East Park United Methodist congregation was called to order by Pastor Tod Maclean at 8:05 P.M. at the United Methodist Church. "Leaning on the Everlasting Arms" was sung. Pastor Tod read a few verses from Matthew, chapter 14, starting at verse 27. He then led the group in prayer. The meeting was turned over to Sidney Sturgess, General Committee Chairman. He spoke on the mission of the church, indicating this was something more than the "self-serving" activities of the church. He brought out that Christ is at the point of greatest human need. We should broaden and deepen our sense of awareness of the claims of the world and human need upon us. We should consider—Are we aware of the mission of the church in East Park? Also—How can we make the best use of the resources which have been entrusted to us?

Tod's words, in a letter to the two congregations, display a similar call to greatness.

Two congregations that have enough faith to commit themselves to the principle of church merger certainly are capable of more than "playing it safe." If we do only that, we will sell ourselves short and come up with something far less than the revitalized Christian witness we have been thinking of and praying for for so long.

Let's be a real church! Let's be bold! We are talking about a "plan of union." Let's have real unity! One church! A new church! And a church who knows who it is and what it wants to do. Let's have real courage *now.* One or two hard decisions dealt with now will avoid dozens of sticky little decisions, year in and year out.

When church members are given a challenge and the means to rise above themselves to meet a higher calling, they often will respond. Merger will probably always be the most difficult church adjustment. But with vision, careful planning, and very careful attention to process, it can be a triumphal experience.

To summarize, key process elements that help to make merger an effective and meaningful experience include:

1. Proposing merger only between congregations whose members belong to similar social contexts.

2. A formal process and structure adequate to define and resolve difficult issues prior to the consummation of the merger.

3. Effective employment of outside resourcers at key points.

4. Adequate and open communication throughout the negotiation period and during the period of integration.

5. Not permitting the need to build an effective organization to override careful attention to the human needs of all persons, especially weaker and nonleader types.

6. A process leading up to the merger that opens the way for integration of the new congregation in the months and years following the merger.

7. Constant restating of a positive vision of the future throughout the negotiating period.

III. The Hazards of Ministry in a Changing Community

Introduction

Many congregations find themselves facing transition today. Metropolitan areas expand to surround rural villages and crossroads with suburban housing. More new social groups displace older residents in city neighborhoods. This transition produces a number of crises for churches. Ministries and leadership effective with the old social group are often not attractive or helpful to new persons moving into the area. When the neighborhood begins to change, the congregation also must make changes in order to continue an effective ministry. Elmwood, a church located in a former rural village, illustrates what happens to a congregation that fails to make the necessary changes and is unable to relate helpfully to the new residents.

The Case

It was much too hot a night for a meeting, and the mood of the board members reflected the weather.

"When I drove by there, those kids were tearing all over the place," one of them said. "You could see it plain as day through the church hall windows. Kids shouldn't behave that way in church. Why, if I'd done that, my father would have tanned my hide." They all agreed.

51

Pastor Tom Brewster felt like a man caught between two worlds. It had all started so simply. He was well-intentioned. He had taken what seemed to him to be logical, Christian action. He had reached out to people who were hurting. He had done what his natural inclinations and his seminary education encouraged him to do.

Walter and Susan Peters had moved with their three children from halfway across the country. They had bought a house outside the village. Their three children had come to Sunday school. On about half the Sundays, they all had come to church service. Then one day Walter went on a business trip and never returned. No one knew what happened to him; he just disappeared.

After Walter was gone, somehow the church in the village didn't offer anything that was really helpful to Susan. Pastor Tom gave her all the support he could, but she really didn't seem to fit anywhere.

Nor did Robert Murphy, the new science teacher in the local high school. Robert was a gentle man. He came from a Quaker background. He was deeply committed to nonviolence. He suffered through the pain of the war in Southeast Asia, and after those years, found himself deeply opposed to nuclear power. Somehow, neither his views nor his life-style seemed to fit in with the Men's Brotherhood, composed of those who had lived in Elmwood for many years.

Eleanor Ortman was another apparent misfit, though it hadn't seemed that way at first. She had married a local policeman. When they first began to attend the Elmwood church, she had participated in the Women's Guild. But the more committed she became to such concerns as Bread for the World, the less time she had for the local guild. Her local concern shifted to gathering surplus food to distribute to needy families in a nearby city.

These were typical of the dozen or so new people Tom Brewster brought together in what came to be called the Wednesday Night Group. What distinguished them most was that they really didn't seem to fit anywhere else. At least half of them didn't even attend Sunday morning services. Pastor

Tom's purpose was not to establish a group over against the existing congregation, though that was, in fact, what resulted. Originally, he thought he was carrying out the wishes of the church board to reach new people. The little church had not done well for a number of years. The former pastor, James Magee, during his twenty years, had been a faithful visitor; but he was not a strong pulpit minister. Pastor Tom, on the other hand, was an excellent preacher. When they had visited with him prior to issuing a call, the church board told him they wanted to reach new people. They said they were hopeful that his strong attention to current issues would help to attract new people. They wanted new people for their church, they said.

At first, things went very well. Not long after Tom arrived, new people began to appear. The word got around. He was an excellent preacher.

Then, toward the end of the first year, there was the incident with Mrs. Eldridge. For thirty-five years, she had taught fourth-grade boys in the Sunday school. One Sunday morning, Jimmy Evans questioned her interpretation of the flood story—he didn't believe there was a real Noah. She nervously informed him he was mistaken and that she, because of her years, had much more wisdom in the matter than he did. A village child would have been quieted. In Jimmy's family, however, everyone had the right, and was encouraged, to ask questions. His father had just moved to the area to join the faculty at a nearby university.

The following Sunday, Jimmy and his father together confronted Mrs Eldridge. She was shocked. The next day, as she sat with Pastor Tom in his study, she asked him to "put them in their place"—which he was not able to do. It was a nasty confrontation for him: Mrs. Eldridge, with her thirty-five dedicated years, thinking him ungrateful because he would not support her against these newcomers; Jimmy and his father, with their feelings that she was out of date and incompetent. Tom hedged—and he lost heavily. Mrs. Eldridge quit teaching. Jimmy dropped out of Sunday school, with the support of his father.

The church board meeting that followed was very strained.

Sixty-year-old board member Henry Johnson, a lifelong resident of the village, spoke for the majority: "If I talked to a Sunday school teacher like that when I was nine years old, my father would have boxed my ears. If Sunday school doesn't teach a child to respect his elders, what good is it, anyway?" Pastor Tom knew better than to argue.

He really agreed with Peter Evans' view, anyway, voiced at the following Wednesday's gathering of the fellowship group. Peter said, "If Sunday school teachers aren't up to date and secure enough to permit legitimate disagreement in their classrooms, then they ought to be replaced. I expect my children to get reliable information and tools with which to define their own working belief system. If they don't get that in Sunday school, it isn't worth attending."

Then something happened that Tom had never expected to happen. He found himself opening his heart to this caring fellowship that night. He was worn from the strain. He told them he felt caught between the old and the new. He told this group of newcomers he really sympathized with their frustration, but he felt powerless.

Group members wanted to support him, and did support him for a time. But as the months went by, their activity in this group provided their only meaningful contact with the church. Gradually criticism mounted, especially against those who did not attend Sunday worship or pledge financial support to the church.

The crowning blow came when Tammy Peters ducked to avoid the volleyball Jimmy Evans threw at her. The adults at the fellowship group that rainy Wednesday night had become so involved in their own conversation that none of them noticed he had brought the ball into the church hall. The ball missed Tammy, but it didn't miss the stack of monogrammed church plates on the cart outside the kitchen door.

"Fourteen plates were broken!" snapped board member Henry Johnson. "My mother was a member of the guild that raised the money to buy those plates. If these new women would get responsibly involved in the guild, like churchwomen are supposed to, they might also see to it that their children are better behaved!"

By itself, the incident probably would not have been significant, but it was yet another aggravation added at the end of a very long series of aggravations. The Wednesday fellowship group never really recovered. They did manage to find someone to make two dozen monogrammed plates almost, but not quite, identical to the ones broken. Their spirits, however, somehow never were mended. After the next summer, they were unable to motivate themselves to meet again.

For his part, Tom kept at his job. He visited and he preached, though the board complained he didn't visit church families enough, and his sermons lacked spark. Tom knew they were right on both counts, nor did he encourage any more new people to participate. He really didn't believe any more that they would find what they wanted in this church. Board members began to complain that he wasn't attracting new members. Other than those few who married into church families, or those children who grew to adulthood and somehow managed to find employment and stayed in the village, they were right. Each year, the financial condition of the church became more and more precarious. With a lack of significant increments, the financial predicament of Tom Brewster's family became equally precarious. When a more open and lucrative charge came his way, he moved on. At the end of his five-year pastorate, except for those who had died, and those who had grown up and left, or married into church families, the same people were participating in the Elmwood church who were there when his ministry began.

What We Can Learn from Elmwood

There are certain key phenomena that leaders in churches facing transition need to understand, in order to help their congregations make critical changes. Leaders also need to recognize that they must act before the opportunity to make these changes is lost.

First, everyone needs to recognize that transition is a threatening experience for any church. The inner life of congregations, like their buildings, is predicated on the assumption that the church will have to face little or no change. When neighborhood transition comes, demanding a great deal of change, the church faces an unnatural and often threatening experience.

Change is difficult for churches for several reasons. First of all, church people tend to approach life normatively. The first question they ask when confronted by options or opportunities is, "Is it right?" In a stable situation, this inherent conservatism serves them well; that which has been proven right time and again is likely to continue to be right. Therefore, the safest course is to keep doing whatever one does in the same way one has always done it. The strongest reference to support any argument or point of view is a reference to tradition or to precedent. In a stable situation, the classic "We've always done it that way before" point of view usually does—and should— carry the day.

When change actually does come, all these natural tendencies are suddenly counterproductive. However, they are still basic life-ways. People have difficulty giving up these old ways, even when they apparently don't work, because they still *seem right*.

Even when someone else points out that the old ways don't work any more, they respond, "They don't work any more because people are not doing what they are supposed to do."

Second, facing transition is a threatening experience for existing church members, because they feel trapped. Consider the pressure, for example, on churches in the fringe of a metropolitan area. Suddenly they find themselves surrounded by a sea of houses and new people. Crowds and traffic disrupt their quiet, traditional way of life. Small businesses lose out to new shopping centers. When the fire whistle blows during the day, few persons respond. Hardly anyone works locally any more. Traditional church supporters grow old. The new people don't seem to care, or to have time for what matters. Church members feel trapped, and even helpless amid the forces of social change.

A second key phenomenon at work in churches in transition is the mistaken hope with which natives reach out to newcomers. Not only do natives view the church as properly unchanging, but they believe that newcomers will support the church basically as it is—that newcomers will affirm the way of life for which the church presently stands. When newcomers do not readily give this support and, especially, if they try to change the church, the natives believe the newcomers are not doing what they are supposed to do. Some natives even feel they should correct the newcomers.

When the Wednesday night study group began in Elmwood, it appeared to the natives that it would be another traditional Bible study group, with the usual family night supper preceding it—both of which were familiar church programs. The atmosphere of the supper would be pleasant, but restrained. The education program would be brief, and with the pastor in charge.

Newcomers, on the other hand, had a different image. They were attracted to the study group precisely because it offered an alternative—something different from the usual well-planned, clergy-dominated church program. The atmosphere was freer, both in the fellowship time and in the study time. As one fellowship group member commented in an interview,

Gradually "backdoor people"—church dropouts and unchurched—became significantly involved. The group seems to attract a certain type of person: the self-starter, the leader, the person with an active opinion, the disaffected. The more passive person, such as the sit-in-the-pew churchgoer, does not seem interested in the group (or perhaps is threatened by it), or if he joins, eventually drops out. I think one of the most significant things about this group is that its members are the types of persons that the normal church program does not usually accommodate.

The group has had a changing relationship with the church. Although the group is officially a program of the church, there have been feelings of exclusion and suspicion on the part of the regular churchgoers, and feelings of being divorced from the rest of the church on the part of group members. I think both factions have tended to concentrate on differences; there is a lack of communication. As the group began to grow, there was the subtle feeling on the part of church members that the group was perhaps stealing members or potential members. There were also questions about what the group contributed monetarily to the church—Are they using our building without pledging anything toward its support?

Thus, natives are left not only with disappointment—the newcomers do not support the church in the way the natives had hoped they would; they also have anxiety—newcomers do not affirm the church's way of life. In fact, they often even seem to undermine it.

The third key phenomenon affecting churches in transition is the fact that natives and newcomers have such dissimilar life experiences. Often, the two groups hardly understand one another at all.

Newcomers do not perceive how deeply they threaten those who have lived all their lives in the village and in the village church. Most of them do not attach the same meaning to change, nor is change such an unusual or upsetting experience for them. Change is more natural and easier for these often better-educated and more mobile persons to accept. One adopts a new way of doing something because it *works* better than the old way, not necessarily because it *is* better. Newcomers are inherently less stable; therefore, all their commitments—geographical, occupational, relational—are more tentative.

Natives, on the other hand, with the overall security of being close to their roots and being surrounded by an extended family and long-standing friends, have great difficulty understanding what it is like to move, to have no place either physically or socially.

One newcomer described his experience at the village church. He knew no one in the village when he moved there with his family. He commuted to the city for employment, so his work gave him no natural avenues to develop relationships within the village. He and his family turned to the church, hoping they would find *friends.* When they appeared on Sunday morning, the church people welcomed them warmly. They told the newcomer and his family how happy they were to see them. They invited him and his wife to Couples Club. They encouraged him to enroll his children in the church school. They said they hoped he and his family would return for worship the following Sunday. Church members said goodby warmly, and then went off to have Sunday dinner with the same friends and/or family they shared it with every Sunday.

On the succeeding Sunday, the newcomer returned to church with his family. The experience of the previous week was repeated, as it was the third week. By the fourth week, he was angry and stayed home.

He said, "I needed friends, people who would include me in their lives and their relationships. The church people were nice enough to me, but they excluded me from what I really needed. They asked me to support their organization. I was lonely."

Most long-standing village residents have never had the security of their family and social relationships disrupted by moving. Often, they simply do not notice the newcomer's need for inclusion and do not reach out to make a place for him in the network of their relationships. Part of the reason the fellowship group became so tightly knit in Elmwood was not only the social similarity of its members, but the inclusion they gave to each other. As one of them commented, "We developed stronger ties and more depth in relationships than we expected . . . The group is bound together by the meaning it gives to the members' lives; they relate to one another in a deeply human way—they give of themselves and receive from others."

Natives also often do not understand how difficult it is to face the tragedies of life far away from any old friends and family. When Susan's husband disappeared, she found herself halfway across the country from her family, forced to turn to people she hardly knew to find the support she needed to survive. She craved people, not just to help her over the immediate crisis; she needed people who would support her for many months, as she attempted to put her life back together.

Natives and newcomers have very different motivations for supporting the church. This is a fourth overall phenomenon affecting churches in transition. Natives support the church because it is there; it is essential to their way of life. Newcomers support the church when it relates effectively to their needs. They view it as one of several institutions that will help to meet their needs.

Newcomers represent a generation of adults, often not socialized in the church, who come to the church primarily for explicitly religious, as opposed to social, purposes. As one of them said in an interview,

We grew up in suburbia and attended church and Sunday school some as kids but gradually drifted away. As adults, we had a neutral feeling toward church. When we first moved to this community, one of our neighbors repeatedly invited us to the Wednesday fellowship group. We weren't very interested but finally agreed rather unenthusiastically to attend. We were immediately attracted to the group by the sense of fellowship and the particular personalities who were there. The group gradually awakened a dormant need and potential in us for spiritual life. We began thinking and talking about it individually and together. After Bible study, we would talk for hours about what we were discovering. We were fascinated by the New Testament. It was our first real exposure to Jesus and the disciples. It was a new type of intellectual stimulation which was very fulfilling.

In contrast to the specific religious purposes for which newcomers often seek out a church, natives, in spite of the religious overtones with which they speak about the church, tend to support the church primarily for the social meaning it has in their lives.

The two approaches are very clear in the conflict over Mrs. Eldridge. For Peter Evans, it was very simple. She was not theologically competent; therefore, she should be replaced. For old-time church members, she deserved to keep her position because she had given thirty-five years of service. For Peter Evans, the church should adjust to meet the needs of his son. For those who sympathized with Mrs. Eldridge, Jimmy Evans should behave himself, out of respect for Mrs. Eldridge and the church she represented.

Community transition is a near traumatic experience for many congregations. Those who carry leadership responsibility in churches facing transition will find several strategies very helpful, even essential.

First of all, lay leaders, and especially pastors, need to deal promptly and effectively with conflict. Unfortunately, neither the lay leaders nor Pastor Tom had the skill to deal with conflict in Elmwood. The lay leaders tended to escalate every conflict. Pastor Tom was easily intimidated; he found it difficult to confront people. He could not deal with anger in either himself or others. He was not able to defuse tension by helping people understand what was happening to them and why they felt the way they did. He took sides. He felt sorry for himself. He could not see through the natives' anger to their fears.

As a result of the inability of either the minister or the lay leaders to deal with conflict, the forces of opposition in Elmwood steadily polarized the congregation, until finally there was no real possibility that the old and the new could live together. Those who disagreed came to view themselves as opponents. They became enemies. What "the others" wanted and needed became not an alternative, but wrong.

If Pastor Tom had employed effective conflict management skills, he could have thwarted this polarization process. He could have helped each group see that they were, in fact, afraid of the other, but were, paradoxically, trapped by their fears, because each needed the other. The natives needed the new people to support their church so it would survive. The new people needed the natives to convince the church to provide the services they wanted.

Pastor Tom could have had an especially effective role as a bridge person. Initially, he was probably the only person in the congregation who understood both the feelings of the natives *and* the feelings of the new people. Each group needed him to help them understand the other. He probably would not have been alone in that task for long. With his encouragement, some native church members could have understood the newcomers' viewpoint. They probably would have participated in the Wednesday night fellowship group. This involvement would have enabled them to discover and to interpret to other natives why this group was meaningful and necessary to the newcomers.

On the other side, Tom could have encouraged some newcomers to take institutional responsibility in the congregation. This experience would have helped them understand the institutional burdens the natives felt, as well as the threat newcomers posed to the natives' life-style. Out of this experience, these newcomers would have been able to interpret to other newcomers the feelings of the natives. Such bridge persons could have provided the links necessary to assimilate newcomers into the existing congregation.

A second strategy important for churches facing transition to follow deals with time: The optimum opportunity to reach newcomers is present only for a limited time. Each church has only a limited time after the newcomers arrive to relate easily to them. If it does not establish itself as an institution that will relate effectively to them within this crucial time period, they will leave that church out of their lives. It will become socially isolated from them. They will view it as an institution appropriate only for natives.

Looking again at Elmwood, we note that the two times when newcomers are most likely to turn toward established churches is immediately after they relocate, when they are trying to make their way into the social system of the community, and again, when they go through a crisis. If newcomers establish themselves socially without that church, or if they work their way through deep crises without that church, they are unlikely to have any future dealings with it.

When a congregation is surrounded by a community in transition, church leaders need to help existing church members recognize that in the short run, the natives hold all the power. Their attitudes and actions either include or exclude the newcomers to the area. On the other hand, church leaders need to help natives realize that in the long run, the newcomers hold the power. Either the church includes them, or it will slowly die out with the natives and the older generations.

Finally, church leaders need to help both long-standing residents and newcomers realize that while some change is inevitable, total change is both unlikely and undesirable. To live in a pluralistic society means that everyone will get something of what he wants but not everything he wants. Thus, existing church members will need to change some aspects of the church's life, but not everything. If they let go of some things they will not have to let go of everything. On the other hand, if they do not let go of anything, they run the risk of losing everything.

In summary, key phenomena that transitional congregations need to consider include:

1. Transition is a threatening experience.

2. Natives tend to look to newcomers with unrealistic anticipation.

3. Natives and newcomers have very dissimilar life experiences and, therefore, find it very difficult to understand one another.

4. Natives and newcomers have different motivations for supporting the church.

Some essential strategies to follow when dealing with transitional congregations are:

1. Deal promptly and positively with conflict.

2. Act while the optimum opportunity to reach newcomers is present.

3. Make necessary changes, but don't attempt to change everything.

Neighborhood transition brings unusual pressure for change to a congregation. Effective leaders can help a congregation recognize the positive opportunities within these pressures for change. They can help existing church members to understand, to accept, and to include newcomers by widening a congregation's programming and broadening its life-style. They can help it not only to survive, but to have an effective ministry in a new day.

IV. The Palatine Cluster— A Surprisingly Mixed Blessing

Introduction

The Palatine Cluster is composed of five small congregations on the fringe of a medium-sized metropolitan area in the northeastern United States. One of the congregations is located in a former rural village, the other four at what was originally a rural crossroads. During the 1960s and into the early 1970s, population grew rapidly in the area served by the churches. These congregations, isolated in their own little hamlets for generations, suddenly found themselves surrounded by hundreds of new houses and several thousand new residents. In an effort to meet the challenges of change, the five congregations and three pastors came together to form a program cluster and a team ministry. During its early years, the Palatine Cluster-team demonstrated powerful possibilities for church renewal and outreach to new persons through a cluster of churches, served by a team of ministers. More recently, however, the cluster has experienced some problems. Most of these apparently stem from its attempt to impose a complex program and staff structure on the simple life-ways of rural people. With its mixture of success and failure, the cluster illustrates the difficulty of meeting the needs of two different social groups simultaneously.

The Case

Stephen Kowalski was surprised at the size of the crowd. There must have been two hundred people gathered in St. Mark's Lutheran Church that fall evening. His first inclination had been to ignore Pastor Kenneth Kirsten's invitation to appear with the other candidates for township office at the Palatine Cluster's Meet Your Candidate Night. Reluctantly, he had changed his mind after a conversation with Fred Janke, local Republican Town Chairman. Fred was on the council at St. Mark's. He told Stephen that the cluster had brought a new day to the five formerly struggling Lutheran churches in Palatine Township. He promised a big crowd would be present to meet the candidates. As Stephen surveyed the large number of people gathered in St. Mark's, he began to believe Councilman Janke's promise that this evening would bring "a church meeting with a difference."

Stephen Kowalski was not the only person in the audience that night who had never been in St. Mark's new church building. Another was John Burchard. Fifteen years ago John had moved with his family into one of the first suburban housing areas to be built in Palatine Township. A construction engineer on the new regional shopping center, and then on project after project, he had watched the area grow from small, isolated villages and crossroads into its now near continuous sea of new homes.

The churches that had dominated the little villages were now almost lost from view amidst the new houses and the shopping centers. New highways passed by them or over them. For most people, the churches were bound to what had been. They had had their heyday in the same era as Hank's Garage across from St. Mark's. Nobody knew how old Hank was. He had begun as a young blacksmith before the turn of the century. When automobiles appeared, he was one of the first to go into the business of putting them together and selling them. When local dealers no longer assembled the automobiles, stubborn Hank gave up the car business. He never tired of telling people that he refused to sell a car he hadn't put together. So for fifty years, Hank had "fixed 'em and gassed 'em." The only place Hank and

John Burchard ever saw each other, that is before tonight, was in Hank's Garage, where John waited willingly—sometimes days—to get his car "fixed right" by Hank's still steady, meticulous hands.

Janice Janke was as pleased as aspiring councilman Kowalski with the size of the crowd. She remembered how very skeptical she had been about this new thing called a cluster when the newly arrived pastor, Kenneth Kirsten, had asked her to serve on the Program Steering Committee for the just-formed cluster of five Lutheran churches. She was one of three representatives from St. Mark's on the PSC, as they called it. The other four churches out in what used to be isolated settlements, each had sent three representatives from their ongoing program committees. These fifteen had joined with the three pastors to compose a team to guide the development of an amazing number of new and often exciting program over the past several years.

As Janice looked about the room, she saw results of the cluster all around her. John Stephens was there with his wife, Janet. They had not been active in any church until two years ago, when the cluster held its first campout over Labor Day weekend. Some thirty families took their tents and trailers to a local campsite. Many of them had remained fast friends ever since. Almost all of them had returned the two succeeding Labor Days. The Stephens' son, Tom, often now stood in the front of this church playing his guitar, singing and accompanying the forty young people whose Christian folksinging had created a sensation throughout the area. Tom had never taken the church very seriously until he and Pastor Kenneth began to play together on the cluster softball team. That friendship carried over into the confirmation class taught by Ken and another cluster pastor as a team, for all the young people of the five congregations that composed the cluster.

The list of new programs that had come and gone during the past three years seemed endless; there had been some thirty of them. One of the most exciting outcomes of the cluster was the willingness of the congregations to try something new, and then let go of it if it turned out not to be effective. This enabled them to find those few programs that were of continuing help to the church members and others in Palatine Township.

Kenneth Kirsten impressed Frederick Janke the first time he met him. Fred Janke was one council member who bridged the gap between the old and the new. He had to bridge it to keep his insurance business alive. Over the past several years, he had added many hundreds of clients to the few old residents who had been served by his father. Every year the margin of profit declined, and the number of clients required to keep an independent insurance agent alive increased. When synod executive Karl Schmidt suggested the cluster-team idea, Fred was one of the first supporters. His enthusiasm made a real difference. His status as a native-born, but obviously successful, businessman made his support of the Palatine Cluster pivotal. He was a natural leader with wide influence.

Fred repected Karl's candid but firm leadership style. Karl openly advocated what he thought would help the five churches in Palatine Township, but he gave those with whom he worked plenty of freedom to make their own decisions. He never imposed his will on a group. He was firm about the necessity to make decisions with dispatch, yet he gave council members ample opportunity to participate and grow comfortable with the decisions they made.

The many potluck suppers held for the sixty council members from all five churches were typical of the open decision-making strategies Karl brought to the Palatine Cluster. The idea of the cluster-team itself was first introduced at one of these potluck meetings. The pattern was very effective. Eating together helped the group become comfortable with each other. They then worked together to develop an agenda for the evening. They talked over suggestions first in small groups, where members of the various councils mixed with one another. Then they met as individual church councils, each council considering carefully the implications of the suggestions for its own congregation and ultimately making its own decisions, which they then came back to share with the entire group.

Council members left these meetings with a common understanding and a common commitment to the decisions they had made. The process is far superior to the usual custom of sending representatives to an area meeting, and then having them come back to their individual councils to justify the decisions. Those at home who have not had the opportunity to discuss the questions involved and who, therefore, have little direct influence on decisions, often do not feel responsible to support them.

On the other hand, following Karl's method, when an entire council worked together with other councils, they were even able to make decisions they knew would be unpopular, but ultimately beneficial for their congregations. They were able to take risks.

These churches needed to take risks. All the congregations, with the possible exception of St. Mark's, would have been described accurately as marginal. In fact, two of them were desperate for survival. Only one church had a pastor. Even so, when Karl Schmidt first proposed a team ministry, the council members hedged at this challenge to local autonomy. But before long, they could begin to see some advantages. The cooperative would bring improved coverage of general pastoral ministry. For example, each minister could visit members of any of the congregations when he discovered them in the hospital. Each pastor could contribute needed specialities to all the churches. The councils in one pair of churches to whom one of the two pastors to be called would be primarily accountable, agreed to look for a pastor with skills in administration. The other two congregations agreed to search for a pastor with special skills in Christian education. Both new ministers would then complement Pastor Robert Adalberg's counseling abilities. Within six months, the search surfaced two very well-qualified candidates who joined with Bob in the team ministry.

There were other advantages of this joint-council approach. Fred Janke often commented about the cost savings possible when five congregations joined to purchase products.

"We saved $300 on fuel oil and $200 on paper in the first year," he said, "and that was just the beginning!"

Of course, the sailing was not always easy. Janice remembered the night Fred came home after the baptism discussion.

For years, the conservative council at St. John's had refused to baptize any but the children of church members.

"How can we fulfill our vows to provide nurture to a child, when his parents aren't even members of our congregation?" one of them said. And for years, many of those whom St. John's council had refused simply went two miles farther down the road to St. Mark's, where the more liberal council was quite willing to leave the issue up to their generally more liberal pastors.

"One of them said, with tears in his eyes, 'You stole our children while we did what was right,' " Fred told his wife. "I never appreciated how deeply they felt until tonight," he went on. "After the joint discussion when we talked to St. Mark's council, we agreed that we can't let ourselves be used by those evading the important question of baptismal vows that St. John's believes they should face. After we sang a hymn together at the end of our meeting, when I told two members of St. John's what we had decided, they shook my hand with tears in their eyes."

The cluster pastors found similar support in their team ministry. Bob described that support:

Those Monday morning meetings we had for nearly six years were one of the most enriching experiences of my ministry. We had our devotions following the lectionary. We shared prayer and talked over the scripture for the week. It really was a boon to my sermon-writing to hear the ideas of the other two pastors. Then we shared difficulties we were having in our churches or special ministry responsibilities we wanted to plan for. The insights and suggestions we were able to give one another were often very helpful. Also, we planned cluster programs and agreed on the leadership roles each of us would take. I don't think I ever want to go back to a "solo" ministry where I work all by myself. The support of colleagues is much too rich an experience.

Of course, it hasn't always been a bed of roses. Working in a team ministry can be a threatening experience, especially at the beginning. Most of us aren't as secure about what we do as we think we are. I'll never forget the difficulty I had when Bob Adalberg's counseling was so helpful to some members of my primary congregation that they became more devoted to him than to me. His effectiveness threatened me. In fact, sometimes it still does.

And not all laypeople have been satisfied with the cluster, either. Older church members, especially, have been bothered by the increased pace and complexity the cluster has brought to our churches. Others feel the loss of closeness or control because they no longer have *a* pastor exclusively serving *their* congregation. A few of the church leaders in the local congregation believe the cluster has just added more work or made their church work more difficult, because now they have to spread themselves over five congregations rather than one. Others believe the cluster has really benefited only the new people who are outsiders, not the five individual congregations.

Fred and Janice Janke also agree that the cluster was far from a perfect experience. They admit that not every program the cluster carried on over the years worked well, nor did every church member find it helpful. Nevertheless, along with most members of the Palatine churches, they continue to believe the gains far outweigh the losses.

Fred summed it up:

The cluster has made a dramatic impact throughout Palatine Township, especially on many people who are not reached by local congregational programs. It significantly upgraded pastoral ministry both for the pastors and most church members. Even now in these years when the individual churches are seeking to assess their own lives in the light of the cluster experience, the benefits of the cluster continue to be felt both within and outside the five congregations of Palatine Township. I'm glad we did it!

What We Can Learn from the Palatine Cluster

There is so much insight which emerges from the Palatine Cluster experience that I will need to divide this section into three parts. First of all, we will review what the cluster made possible. Second, we will analyze factors that made the cluster successful. Third, we will point out difficulties that emerged to plague the cluster and suggest strategies others can follow, either to deal with these difficulties as they emerge, or to avoid them altogether.

What the Cluster Made Possible

This combination of a cluster of congregations served by a team of ministers has great potential to improve the program life of smaller congregations. It makes the resources of each of the congregations available to all of them. It brings the resources of all the pastors to all the congregations. The results of this merging of resources in the Palatine Cluster are very impressive.

First, the cluster added a great deal of new program, and much of it was of very high quality. The following list of programs is based on a report the cluster released at the beginning of its fourth year. Programs which can be attributed directly to the cluster included:

Cluster Lenten series
Three-church summer program for youth and children
Congregational potlucks
Church picnics
Five-church newsletter
Meet Your Candidate town forum
Thanksgiving Eve service
Square dance and masquerade party
Bible study series
Pulpit exchange
Combined program for young people and parents
Training conference for church elders
Palm Sunday cantata
Preparation for marriage symposium
Campouts
Workcamp for young people
Special services on Ascension, Pentecost, Christmas Eve
Task force on social concerns
Family enrichment program
Music workshop
Youth folksinging choir
Employment of a minister of music to serve the five
    congregations
Touring drama group
Summer outdoor worship services

For a number of reasons, the quality of these programs was far higher than could have been achieved by any of the individual congregations or pastors working alone. The large base of persons the cluster afforded attracted and provided the means to pay for outside speakers and other program resources. The team ministry enabled that minister with an ability related to a particular program to service that program for all five congregations. The cluster confirmation class is a good example of what the shared leadership made possible. Dividing the responsibilities enabled each pastor to conduct those classes which most nearly matched his talents. The reduced work load gave him more time to prepare for those classes he did conduct. The increased staff time available, as well as the outside resources, enabled the pastors to extend the duration of the class; they could cover more material. Having more young people in the class raised the quality of the discussion. The greater variety of church activity to which the young people were exposed by the cluster gave them a deeper and broader understanding of the church.

Second, new program introduced by the cluster attracted new people both from within and from beyond the church membership. Working together, the churches were able to enter entirely new areas to relate to interests or special concerns of persons who either had never participated in, or who were on the fringes of the congregations. A good example is the Meet Your Candidate night mentioned previously. A report written following the first Meet Your Candidate night illustrates the high quality of these evenings.

The chairperson of each party was asked if his candidate would participate. Specific questions, time limits, ground rules were planned with a moderator (an attorney who is a member of a cluster church). Mimeographed copies were sent to each candidate through the party chairpersons. News releases spelling out the questions were also distributed. Each candidate was given ten minutes to respond to these questions:
1. State your background or qualifications for this office.
2. What is important for this office to deal with in the next five years?
3. What is important in zoning, taxation, industry, water and sewer service in our township?
The moderator was strong and humorous. When the floor was open, he kept the discussion on the topic; when candidates broke

the ground rules he clarified and made them move on. The nonoffice-holder spoke first, which helped to center the talk on issues, rather than on personalities.

Some criticized, saying the program should not be held in the church because it was political. When it was suggested that it be moved to the firehouse, others said, "No, let's keep the atmosphere as high as possible."

One of the pastors reporting on new programs said, "Basically, the outsiders liked what they saw. The majority felt the events they attended were beneficial to the community as a whole. Typical comments I heard were:

The cluster adds more of everything.

It brings a variety of talented people.

It broadens the perspective of local people.

It's nice to see young people involved.

It fosters community spirit.

It eliminates petty competition."

Third, the cluster, through its team ministry, raised the quality of ministry. It did this in a number of ways. First, it broadened the coverage of ministry. One minister visiting in the hospital would visit not only those members from his own congregation who happened to be there, but he would look for members from all five congregations. This cooperation avoided unnecessary duplication of effort, particularly as church members grew to accept the ministry not simply of their own pastor, but of all three pastors of the team. A second benefit of team ministry was that all the congregations could enjoy the unique specialities of each pastor. One pastor excelled at counseling, a second at administration, the third as an educator. Each was able to practice his specialty across five congregations. Finally, the congregations gained added variety. Church members were unanimous, for example, in their praise of frequent pulpit exchanges by pastors in the cluster.

Fourth, the cluster resulted in much greater efficiency and economy for the participating congregations. They centralized their purchasing; they centralized the production of printed material; they were able to obtain a bulk mailing permit; they developed a joint newsletter which gave news both of cluster activities and of the individual congregations. They were able to employ a parttime secretary.

In summary, clustering for these churches resulted in greater quantity and quality of program, more variety of program, participation of more and different people, more available resources, a wider range of ministerial talent and experience, much greater efficiency and economy. None of the churches could have achieved these gains on its own.

Key Factors Contributing to the Success of the Cluster-Team Ministry

My study of the Palatine Cluster-team ministry indicates there are identifiable factors that contributed to the success of that cooperative effort and that must be present for any similar attempt to succeed.

First, the entry into a complex cooperative effort among several congregations needs to be carefully designed and executed. The Palatine Cluster illustrates how an effective entrance design can be carried out. A judicatory executive visited each congregation individually, met with the council in an unpressured environment, explained the advantages and some of the disadvantages of the proposed cluster team ministry. He gave the council members adequate opportunity to work through any reservations they had concerning the cluster. The councils then met jointly on several occasions. These joint meetings gave them the opportunity to explore the cluster-team ministry as a total group, to test their perceptions against the perceptions of others, and to come to know and trust council members in the other congregations *before* they committed themselves to the cluster. Two of the three pastors who became members of the team ministry were invited to serve their primary congregations with the understanding that they would also serve on a team ministry. They entered their pastorates with talents and expectations that strengthened the cooperative ministry. These careful steps taken in the months before the formation of the cluster were fundamental to its success.

The second strength of this cluster was its composition. It was formed from strong, as well as weak, congregations. Clustering is rarely successful when all the congregations involved are weak. It amounts to a pooling of intense problems, with no resources to deal with the probl .ms. The problems then tend to become magnified. On the other hand, clustering that mixes weaker churches with stronger churches brings the resources of the stronger churches to help the weaker churches and gives talented persons within both weak and strong churches the opportunity and challenge of greater ministry.

A third factor contributing to the strength of the Palatine Cluster was its well-designed, formal structure. The process of clustering, like all organizational development, involves facing difficult decisions. The process leading up to these decisions and the decisions themselves strain the organization of the existing congregations and the relationships within those congregations. A cluster structure that insures stability and provides adequate communication is almost indispensable. The Palatine Cluster provided a stable structure and adequate communication in a number of ways.

First of all, the councils of *all* the congregations involved met at least twice yearly for planning and decision-making. These meetings, beginning with potluck suppers, provided the opportunity for council members to meet one another informally, encouraging the development of trust relationships. The agenda of the evening provided two essential group mixes within which to process questions and make decisions. Council members met first in small groups, each of which included council members from all the congregations involved. This mix allowed members of each council to test their ideas and to hear the views of council members from all the other councils on whatever issues confronted the churches. Then in the second part of the evening, each council met alone. Members of each council could discuss the questions at hand in the light of their just-gained knowledge of the views of the other councils on these issues. As they made decisions, they were aware of the implications of these decisions for themselves, and for the other churches as well.

At the end of the evening, each council shared its decisions with the other councils. A general discussion followed. Most of the time, differences were resolved in the general discussion. When differences could not be resolved, the whole group was often able to agree on more than one way of proceeding, or that a particular program would be developed only by those congregations who were interested in it.

A second joint structure was the Program Steering Committee. This committee was composed of two adult leaders active in the major programs of each congregation and one young person, also an active leader in the program life of each congregation, plus the three pastors. This eighteen-member PSC met monthly. It reviewed existing program, looked for needs that were not being met, proposed new program to address those needs, and either planned new program itself, or formed task forces of interested, talented persons to plan it. The PSC functioned structurally as a subcommittee of the joint church councils. At times, it received program ideas from the five church councils. Whenever it proposed program that involved cooperation of the churches, it presented these proposals to a joint meeting of the church councils for discussion and approval.

The Monday morning meeting among the pastors formed a third ongoing formal structure. These meetings provided regular opportunity for the pastors to evaluate ongoing program, to check details of program development with each other, to make needed changes, and to solve problems that arose during the day-to-day execution of joint program.

With these three ongoing structures, the Palatine Cluster provided the means for action of the three types of persons who carry responsibility for program development and implementation in congregations. In any congregation or group of congregations, whenever a new program is proposed, or someone raises a question about an existing program, the formal structure must provide opportunity to address these different kinds of concerns.

Program leaders look at a new program with these questions: Will it work? Will I be able to use it? In other words, they need to answer questions of effectiveness.

Board members raise policy questions such as: Will we be able to afford it? Who will be offended by it? Is it a safe program for this congregation? They need to be able to answer questions relating to policy.

Pastors need to answer administrative questions: What will it be like to be responsible for this program month after month and year after year? Will it be difficult to recruit leadership, and what will I have to do if I can't recruit leadership?

The formal structure of a congregation, and especially the formal structure of a cluster, needs to provide channels through which policy leaders, program leaders, and pastors can all address their unique concerns. The fact that the Palatine Cluster's structure provided those effective means for all three groups is one reason it was so successful.

A fourth reason was its excellent communication system. In any organizational development, particularly an intricate organizational development like the cluster-team ministry, good communication is crucial.

The large number of persons from all the congregations who were involved in the formal structure of this cluster helped to insure open and thorough communication. Approximately six dozen people were significantly involved, either in the joint council meetings or the program committee. In each congregation, a large number of members had firsthand information. The presence of so many well-informed persons helped to keep misunderstanding and misinformation at a minimum.

In the early months of the cluster, the congregations also agreed to publish a joint newsletter. This newsletter contained information about cluster activities and also information about program in each of the individual congregations. An information survey conducted in the third year of the cluster indicated that 65 to 70 percent of the church members got their information about the cluster directly from the newsletter. Respondents also indicated that they read not just the general sections of the newsletter and the sections which pertained to their own congregation, but the sections which pertained to the other congregations as well. As a result, members of each church had real appreciation for the life and concerns of the other four congregations.

A fifth factor strengthening this cluster was the increase in satisfaction and opportunity the pastors received from the team ministry.

The pastors were unusually effective for a number of reasons: They were free to spend more time in those aspects of the ministry for which they felt exceptionally well-qualified, or that they simply liked best. They also found real support in the reduced duplication and greater efficiency the team ministry provided. Each pastor could give more time to those aspects of ministry for which he was best qualified, which resulted in a net gain of time and energy. Also, agreements to include parishioners from all five parishes in such activities as hospital calling made for more efficiency; when a pastor found a church member in a hospital for a routine medical problem, the parishioner would often accept his visit in lieu of a visit from the pastor of his own particular congregation.

Perhaps most significant of all was the ability the ministers developed to give personal support to one another. They grew to respect, to like, and to trust one another. The experience of personal support helped them to persist in the team ministry, even in the face of misunderstanding and criticism which emerged from some church members. When an independent evaluator asked the members of the team ministry how it had been of help to them personally, one minister spoke simply of friendship; another, of "the resources in the other team members" as being helpful; and the third, that "the proximity to another team member day-by-day" was a help. However, all three mentioned that "having someone to talk with" was a most significant factor.

The wide acceptance and support of the team ministry among lay people in the five congregations represents the sixth significant strength of the Palatine Cluster. To survive through time, a team ministry must not only be beneficial to the congregations and team members, but must be perceived as being beneficial, both to the team members and to the church members.

In the Palatine Cluster, church members by and large appreciated the benefits the ministers enjoyed from working together. One church member summed up his views by saying that it "helps the ministers to be able to talk their troubles over with one another." Another member said, "By himself, a minister might go dry. Instead, he is constantly exposed to new viewpoints." Church members saw the team ministry as a supportive and broadening experience for the ministers and the congregation. Their affirmation was very significant.

A seventh strength of the Palatine Cluster was the ability of its leaders to confront painful issues directly and without delay. For example, when the councils realized that there was deep disagreement, especially between two congregations over the matter of membership criteria and requirements for baptism, they arranged for a conference on membership policy and sacraments. The conference provided opportunity for council members to listen to one another and to resolve their disagreements. We have seen previously that unresolved disagreements about basic concerns can plague a joint effort, rendering program and leadership ineffective. The ability to resolve conflict effectively was an important strength of this cluster.

An eighth factor contributing to the strength of the cluster was the large number of persons who supported cluster programs. The increased number of active participants had a snowballing effect. As one person put it, it was good to be "in fellowship with people who normally wouldn't be seen." Others who attended cluster events felt the occasions were marked by more enthusiasm and feeling than a single church could muster by itself. Most people approved the large attendance at cluster events, the general feeling being that the bigger the crowd at any event, the better it was. As one member from the smallest congregation termed it, he was "tired of half-empty churches" and felt it was a treat to see "a packed house." A turnout of a crowd, instead of the faithful few, was encouraging both to the producers and to the people who attended programs. It gave church members a sense of "we are making it."

Small churches need some successes. Often the minister or lay people who produce a program are discouraged because only a few attend. The presence of a crowd, when participants from five churches were pooled, was a stimulating factor all by itself.

Cluster events also helped attendance in the individual churches to some degree, simply because they got more people out. When people came to high-quality cluster events, they were stimulated. This stimulation increased their confidence in the churches, and this increased confidence and enthusiasm spilled over into a general increase in churchgoing activity.

A ninth factor contributing to the effective strength of the Palatine Cluster was the effective role of the judicatory. Judicatory staff helped with the design of the cluster. They helped to initiate the cluster by providing process leaders who visited with the five congregations individually and then assumed leadership in meetings of the five councils. Judicatory staff offered program suggestions and helped design particular programs when the Program Steering Committee identified areas of need. Judicatory staff provided evaluation and suggestions for changes in meetings with the councils, program committee, and the team ministry. The judicatory also furnished a small amount of dollar support, both to stimulate new program and to defray some of the costs of administration. Also, by maintaining an interest in the ongoing progress of the cluster, the judicatory provided external accountability—an interested third party, asking from time to time how things were going and whether, in fact, the congregations and their leaders were doing what they had said they would do.

A tenth strength of the Palatine Cluster was the enlarged vision it gave to members of the five congregations. It helped church members to see that there was more to the church than just what went on in their particular small congregation. Events beyond their own congregation provided opportunity for extended ministry, and also provided a supply of resources. As time passed, some church leaders came to see that they did not have to solve all the problems and carry all the responsibilities by themselves.

In the words of one cluster pastor, church members "seem to feel much more free to go back and forth for different things, different programs, even for a worship service, no matter where it happens to be. They feel they can go back and forth now and be a part of it. They know a lot of people in the other congregations. In that way, the cluster experience has really been a melting pot."

Difficulties That Stemmed from the Cluster

As we might expect, all experiences in the cluster were not positive. After four years of intense activity, the cluster moved into a period of de-emphasis, a time of regrouping, of individual congregations coming to terms with their own identity in light of the cluster experience. The outcome of this time of question asking has been a modified cluster, with three congregations continuing to share significantly with each other, while two congregations chose a more tenuous relationship. A careful evaluation of the Palatine Cluster yields some insight into these difficulties, as well as revealing some strategies which, if followed, would help avoid similar pitfalls in future clusters and team ministries.

The frustrations fall into four areas: first, difficulties growing out of the experience of the team ministry; second, disappointments for the congregations; third, pitfalls which emerged from the very success of the cluster; and fourth, difficulties that resulted from a lack of integration of the cluster into the ongoing life of the five congregations.

Turning first to the frustrations the team ministry experienced: *working in the team ministry turned out to be surprisingly threatening to the pastors.* "None of us anticipated how difficult it would be for ministers to move into a team style. Ministers are educated to work alone, to be self-sufficient and independent. Working in a team is a difficult and sometimes threatening experience."

Working in the team produced accountabilities to which participating ministers were not accustomed. Their activities were constantly scrutinized by peers with educated eyes. Moreover, the effectiveness of one pastor in areas where another pastor felt weak turned out to be almost devastating at times.

"When Bob Adelberg's counseling abilities were celebrated to me by members of my own congregation in glowing terms," one of the other pastors commented, "I got an awful feeling in the pit of my stomach. It was *very* difficult for me to accept the fact that he could help them where I couldn't. I felt I ought to be able to help them in all respects, that my lack of ability was clear evidence of personal failure." Only strong relationships among team members and, at times, the help of skilled counselors, enabled the team to stay together to work through these feelings.

Second, if the ministers were uncomfortable at times, so were members of the congregations. Sometimes the team ministry was a threat to the congregations. Some church members were uncomfortable with a style of ministry that broke the exclusive relationship of pastor and congregation. They resented a stand-in for their pastor in times of crisis—for example, in the hospital. Would the team ministry spell the end of local church autonomy? Would the pastor who taught a joint communicant's class, for example, develop loyalties to himself among class members? If so, would young people emerge from the class more committed to him than to their own congregation?

Still others reacted adversely to the team ministry's decision to list a single telephone number. Designed by the ministers to insure that one pastor could always be reached at any time by any member of any congregation, some church members saw the team ministry becoming like a group medical practice. The new style felt impersonal, compared to the old style of one pastor to one congregation. It took great persistence and constant interpretation for the pastors to establish the values of the team ministry to many critics. Some remained unconvinced.

Critics also pointed out some negative effects the cluster had on congregations as institutions. *First, some church members felt attention was given to the cluster largely at the expense of the individual congregations.* Older church members and longer residents in the community were least enthusiastic about the benefits of clustering. The cluster was novel. It attracted a lot of attention and demanded much time. Its greater size tended to overshadow the individual congregations. Some church members wondered: Will everyone eventually forget how vital and important the local churches are?

Thus while the cluster, with its dynamic new program, was drawing many excited participants, it appeared to be doing so at very great expense, in the eyes of many older residents and longstanding members of the individual congregations. A few church members even looked upon the cluster as the beginning of an attempt to shut down the small congregations. They persisted in this belief, in spite of repeated denials on the part of pastors, council members, and representatives of the regional judicatory.

Probably these feelings emerge out of long years of anxious struggle to keep churches open in the face of near impossible challenges, and are typical among members of small congregations. Church members who live year after year in a steadily worsening situation, believing that sooner or later someone or something will shut down their congregations, eventually come to feel that *any* change is the beginning of the end. For this reason, it is important for leaders in a cluster involving marginal congregations to give at least as much attention to the congregations and their needs as they do to the cluster. Leaders need to make clear repeatedly that the purpose of a cluster is to *supplement* local activity. If a cluster is, in fact, a first step toward a merger, that should be stated openly.

The Palatine Cluster met with wide approval when it focused on special events, or the needs of special groups, or programs that require so many people that the local churches could not have produced them alone. On the other hand, when the cluster even appeared to threaten the ongoing church life, deeply meaningful to those members who had supported the individual congregations at great personal expense for many years, they became increasingly anxious. Once threatened, they became suspicious about every cluster activity.

Some of the heaviest criticism of the Palatine Cluster came from those who felt it was not necessary. This is particularly true of some members of the stronger churches involved in the cluster. At times, these churches contributed an "unfair" share of leadership and resources to the cluster. When attention to the cluster appeared to be given at the expense of attention to individual congregations, these church members became very concerned. Insofar as they viewed the cluster as a threat to their churches, they saw participation by their congregations as unduly expensive. To counteract these feelings in a cluster, leaders need to give as much attention to the needs of the individual congregations as they do to the cluster and its needs.

We turn now to a second difficulty. *From the beginning, the cluster did not give enough attention to the differences among the congregations.* To be successful, a cluster must recognize the differences among the congregations that compose it.

In the Palatine Cluster, the level of activity in two of the congregations was greater than it was in the other three. The leaders, especially, in those two congregations ended with a feeling that they were carrying the burden for the rest. One congregation is larger and conceivably could have survived well without the cluster. Those congregations which entered the cluster with effective program and with strong leaders found themselves spread thinner by the cluster.

One member of such a church said that workers in his congregation "wind up having to do everything; it's like having two churches." Another member of a strong church was even more blunt: "The other churches do not carry the load; we do all the work." Another commented similarly, "Less active churches expect the cluster to do everything for them."

Actually, there is probably no way to distribute the work load equitably in a cluster. A church cannot produce upon demand talented leaders or church workers with the needed physical and mental capabilities. Some of the churches needed the cluster precisely because they lacked such people. Possibly the most serious mistake in the early months of the cluster was promising too much. Such promises built false expectations that the cluster would bring *equal* benefits to the congregations.

In preparing congregations for clustering, it is important to develop realistic expectations. This is especially true for the stronger congregations. They can be encouraged to view their effort as an investment in ministry to the other congregations. While it might be more difficult initially to recruit congregations to cluster on this basis, it would also prevent anger and disappointment, and even disillusionment, when the cluster turns out to be more costly than beneficial.

We now turn to several difficulties which emerged from the success of the cluster. In fact, we can call them the hazards of success.

While successful programs with large crowds in attendance are dynamic, exciting, happy, rewarding experiences for many people, many others feel very uncomfortable in a large group. Increased size often ran counter to the values and emotional expectations of most of the members of the existing churches that composed the cluster. *Large scale programs that attracted new people to the Palatine Cluster turned out to be alienating experiences for many existing church members. The difficulty this increase in size poses for many church members is the first hazard of success.*

Many small churches were never very much larger than they are today. Most of those who participate in small congregations both want and *need* a small-scale church. With the general attitude prevalent in our society today that success is measured by size or scale, it is easy to forget that some people do not function well in a large crowd. The fact that small congregations, which were supportable institutions in the past, are now less able to survive economically than they were fifty years ago, does not alter the peculiar needs or desires of many of those who participate in them. The cluster, instituted to aid the survival of the small congregations and to attract outsiders not active in the congregations, turned out to be a difficult experience for many existing church members.

The most common criticism from existing church members was that cluster programs were too big. They had a sense of being lost in the crowd; size was overwhelming. Even as some were being attracted by the content of cluster programs, they were being alienated by the fact that these programs occurred in what was for them an unfamiliar and uncomfortable church setting.

Added to the problem of size was a second difficulty which stemmed from the success of the cluster—the problem of pace. The cluster often increased the pace of life in the congregations. Many existing members, particularly those who were responsible for carrying the burden of program leadership, found the increased pace disagreeable and difficult to maintain. There was so much more to do, and it all had to be done so quickly.

In any clustering, it is important to take into account the usual institutional experience out of which people in small churches come. Small churches are not only not big, they are generally not fast-paced. Even those church members who sought the Palatine Cluster, once they were in the middle of it, at times found its fast pace disagreeable and difficult to maintain.

The third pitfall engendered by successful clustering is more subtle. When things are going so well, it is easy to overlook the ongoing need for human support. The rewards of success appear to be sufficient to sustain those who are investing so deeply in making a cluster a successful experience. As time passed, the continuing investment of effort necessary to maintain the Palatine Cluster became an exhausting experience for many. They spoke often of "being spread out too thin." Leaders began to drop out, not because they had lost interest, but because they were worn out.

Working in a setting where both scale and pace are unfamiliar is a costly experience. If pastors and judicatory consultants are prepared ahead of time for the human costs of the cluster, they can provide more adequate resources to minister to the human needs of those who are giving so much to make it successful.

A fourth difficulty arising out of the success of the cluster was the premature withdrawal of judicatory resources. Judicatory staff withdrew from active facilitation during the second year, believing that continuing such a role would foster dependence. This withdrawal proved both premature and harmful.

Judicatory leaders need to be very careful in distinguishing between healthy and unhealthy interventions in local church life. They also need to realize that interventions, unhealthy at one stage, may be very necessary at another. At the beginning of an organizational change, local leaders usually lack needed insight and information, as well as the courage to launch out alone in unfamiliar territory. At this stage, outside consultants can furnish the insight. They can point to others who have taken similar risks successfully, to provide needed encouragement. It is true that to continue in such a role beyond the early stages of a cluster fosters unhealthy dependency. Local leaders do need to learn to fly on their own.

However, there are definite roles that judicatory or other outside consultants need to play on a continuing basis. One of the more important of these is to call local leaders to account periodically. Outside resourcers, who return from time to time to ask local leaders what they have been doing, encourage local leaders to ask themselves the same question. They stimulate leaders to examine their effectiveness more closely than they might on their own. Also, those engaged in a complex, difficult organizational change continue to need additional insights and additional resources beyond those they are able to provide for themselves. The fact that they are responsible and capable of directing that organizational change does not eliminate their continued need for outside resourcers.

When the synod withdrew its resources, instead of changing to patterns of resourcing more appropriate to the advanced stages of the cluster, *legitimate* needs for outside resourcing went unmet. Then when local leaders floundered, it appeared they were not capable of directing the affairs of the cluster. Actually, they were. Had they been given appropriate continuing insight and direction by outside resourcers, they would have been much more effective.

A final unanticipated difficulty is the fact that even after several years, it proved almost impossible to integrate the cluster into the social systems of the existing congregations. We have already noted that cluster programs attracted newer residents, people on the edges of the existing congregations; they tended to be younger, better educated, and so forth. On the whole, they were different from many participants in the congregations which formed the cluster. Cluster leaders assumed that these new persons would eventually relate to the existing congregations. A final surprise was that they did not. Even after years of participation, many of those who were attracted by cluster programs did not transfer their commitment to *any* of the existing congregations. The cultural gap between new suburban residents and those who are longstanding church members is very wide. The cluster hid that gap for a time, but it did not eliminate it. New residents who responded to cluster programs often found themselves socially so different from participants in the existing congregations that they were unable to establish meaningful relationships.

Realistically, we have the right to ask whether it is possible for small churches *ever* to meet the needs of new suburbanites. A cluster may, in fact, need to be their congregation. If so, clusters or other new forms of congregational life need to exist *permanently* side by side with small churches, to offer an alternative, larger, and different church experience for the new people. It is probably no more realistic to expect those attracted by a cluster to find participation in the small congregation a desirable and helpful experience than it is to expect existing members of a small congregation to find participation in the larger cluster a helpful and desirable experience.

What to Expect When Churches Cluster

As we look back over the years of the Palatine Cluster, several overall insights into the phenomenon of clustering itself emerge. They tell us something about what we can expect when churches cluster.

1. Clustering will bring an increased quantity and quality of program.

2. Clustering will bring uneven benefits to congregations and participants. Recognize that not everyone will want to participate in the same way, and also that not all churches will want to participate in the same way. Don't promise benefits to everyone. Some simply may find clustering to be an expensive investment in service.

3. Clustering will attract new people and will alienate some existing participants. The same developments that attract new persons (such as greater numbers, increased pace, and size of programs) will likely alienate existing participants.

4. Those attracted by cluster programs will not automatically join one of the individual congregations which compose the cluster. Some persons attracted by the cluster will probably never join a congregation in the cluster. Their continuing participation will depend on the continuing effectiveness of the cluster.

5. Pastors who serve a cluster in a team ministry will be likely to find the experience both exhilarating and threatening. They will experience both gains and losses.

6. A cluster that is simply tolerated on top of existing church program, but never recognized to be as legitimate as the individual congregation, is not likely to have any permanence. Unless existing church members come to see the value of cluster programs, even when these programs do not benefit them directly, they will not be likely to give cluster programs longterm support.

7. The success of the cluster will be stimulating, especially to congregations where nothing successful has occurred in some time. The exhilaration will fade, and there must be a heavy investment to support the human needs of cluster leaders, in order to maintain necessary enthusiasm.

Clustering can be a dynamic, exhilarating, extremely beneficial, and very demanding experience for churches who choose to attempt it. The program benefits, as we have seen, can be immense. The gains and opportunities for ministry, both for the pastors and church members, can be very significant. But church leaders need to recognize that church members and congregations will find clustering a mixture of gains and losses, and that some will lose at least as much as they gain. To minimize the losses and maximize the gains, a cluster demands continuing attention by leaders who are both committed and sensitive.

V. A New Church That Didn't Make It

Introduction

Newton, a new church development field in a growing suburb, within three years became identified as "the new little church that won't make it." The founding pastor's leadership method encouraged a church style that is severely restrictive, as well as unsuited to a suburban context. The intimate fellowship the founding pastor encouraged was unable to grow beyond the few dozen initial members he attracted. When financial pressures on the congregation became intolerable, the pastor sought help from his regional judicatory. Ineffective resourcing by the judicatory, especially employment of a consultant who affirmed the inappropriate style of the congregation, worsened the church's predicament.

The Case

Executive Presbyter MacArthur:

We all thought Rick would make it big. I first met him seven years ago when I came on the presbytery staff. It was the day after he'd been to a "congregational meeting" of the Newton church.

"Now, if you really want to see what we're like," Pastor Rick said, "you should have been there last night and seen our congregation gathered around tables drinking wine in the banquet room of Marty's Steak House. It was like a family reunion. You will rarely see a group of people who are as easy with each other or who care about each other more than these people do. Anybody watching them can see how close they are. After we had supper together, we sat around and talked about our church program—whether we were doing what we want to do, how it's going, and made a few plans for the year ahead. Most of all, we affirmed each other. We do that every time we get together. That's what people need most of all in the suburban madhouse in which we live. At the end of the evening, we shared communion. The warmth of the wine from the common chalice symbolized the warmth of caring we have for each other.

"That fellowship is about the only church 'organization' we have. You always have to put the word 'organization' in quotes when you talk about our church. When I came here two years ago to start this congregation, I said to myself, 'The one thing I'm not trying to have is a lot of organization. That's what kills churches—committees upon committees that do nothing except sap people's time and energy.' So we don't have any, and I mean *any*. When something needs doing or deciding, I call together a few people and we decide it or we do it. Once a year, we have a get-together of the whole congregation; and we talk about everything. That's our evaluation and our planning. I know some people wouldn't like a church like ours, but there's plenty of churches around with committees they can go to.

"That kind of church is not for me, though. I'll never go back to that. We are more like the smalltown church where I began my ministry than the cold, formal, big-organization churches we see all around us. We know each other, and we care about each other. We often share meals together. It's just as natural for us to have a cookout as it is for us to pray together. I know every one of the six dozen members of my congregation like they were my own family."

Rick really impressed me in that first meeting. "He's one to watch," I said to myself. And I watched him. Every so often I would stop around during the next couple of years to see how he was doing. He always told the same stories but, as time passed, with less enthusiasm. The names of the people he talked about never changed, and gradually I began to realize that was because there weren't any new people. The statistical reports told the story. The first year the congregation ended up with thirty-seven members; the second year they reported seventy-two; the third year, seventy-six; the fourth year, sixty-nine.

Then one day he showed up without his familiar smile. The bounce was gone; he was stuck—temporarily, of course—he said. The church had somehow accumulated $6,000 in unpaid bills. The fifth year of the church's life was about to begin. During that year, they were committed to begin paying on the mortgage on their new building. The presbytery had agreed to cover it until then. What they needed was some breathing space, he said, a little time to get themselves together—and also for the presbytery to cosign with them on a note at the bank so they could pay off the $6,000 in accumulated bills.

I was glad to see him. I knew they needed to come close to the forecast of two hundred twenty members by the end of the fifth year to make it financially, and they were a long way from that. They would be lucky to have a hundred. As we talked, we agreed that some of the difficulty could be attributed to "the times." Suburbs at the end of the sixties and the beginning of the seventies were not like suburbs at the end of the fifties and the beginning of the sixties.

But whatever might be the causes of its dilemmas, clearly the congregation needed help. We were all headed for financial disaster if this church didn't go. For some reason, its vibrant, dynamic, close fellowship was not attracting any additional members, and we needed to find out why.

We agreed the problem was not simple, and that we needed someone with expertise to help us. Enter Jack Pearse. He seemed ideal. After eight brilliant years as a pastor (in the late fifties and early sixties, by the way), he decided he wanted to make his talents available to a wider constituency than he could serve in a single congregation. He also decided he needed some tools he didn't have, so he took a master's degree in administration at one of the finest graduate schools in the country. He specialized in human relations and oganizational development. His academic record was impressive. Besides that, he and Rick were the best of friends. Rick was very comfortable about asking Jack to work in what was potentially an embarrassing situation to him.

So we made a contract with Jack in which we gave him a free hand. We had the utmost confidence in him.

The first thing he did was to ask a dozen or so key leaders in the new congregation to make an extended weekend retreat with him. The purpose of the retreat was for them to get to know him and to become comfortable with him, so they would level with him about the problems of the congregation and their feelings.

His analysis and prescription for the Newton church, formulated over the next several weeks, were swift. Church leaders were tired. The pressures of the small congregation were too burdensome for them when added to job pressures and family pressures. During the retreat, and in the weekly meetings of the "planning group" following the retreat, person after person shared with the group the difficulties he or she was attempting to cope with.

"We can't expect these people to give out to the church when they have so many unmet needs of their own," Jack told us. And he assured us it wouldn't take him long to mold them into an effective support group, after which, as they got their needs met, they would be able to attack the problems of the congregation with the new energy they would find.

Well, eighteen months and several thousand dollars later we terminated the consultant. It was all very painful. We suspected for several months that he wasn't helping the situation. Moreover, he and Rick had an increasing number of encounters, especially as he became closer to members of the congregation. Two months after we terminated Jack, Rick resigned to accept a call to a smalltown church. That's not to say Jack did nothing. As a matter of fact, several members of the groups he formed—from a human point of view—improved significantly and functioned much better as human beings than they did previously. But while they grew emotionally, they didn't grow into responsibility for the Newton church. As a matter of fact, most of them left the Newton church.

In the meantime, the unpaid bills have accumulated. At the end of the seventh year, the congregation numbers seventy-eight members. Several key lay leaders have left. The church has no pastor. Fortunately, the land and building are zoned commercial. If we sell both, we will probably break even, though the dollars we realize will not make up for the huge expenditure of energy, heartache, and disappointment over the last seven years.

I know that it seems like absolute failure to talk about selling the property, but Rick was so key in the life of this congregation; now that he's gone, no one knows quite what to do. There is no formal organization; no one knows who's responsible for anything. We have neither trained leaders nor any structure to which to turn, and we don't have resources to build either one. So the best course, indeed the only course of action, seems to be to get out of it altogether.

What We Can Learn from Newton

Newton poses a dilemma. Why did this promising field plateau after two years of growth and eventually take a turn for the worse? Why was the judicatory unable to interrupt the decline?

If we look back over this case, we see several key misjudgments. Decision that leaders made concerning leadership style, church organizational style, and eventually, the role the judicatory would play, set this congregation up for disaster, and after it was headed in that direction, almost insured that the disaster would occur. While it is true that the opportunities for church growth were not, as one of the characters in the case indicates, so promising in the late sixties and early seventies as they were in the middle fifties through the early sixties, most of the causes of Newton's downfall can be traced much more to decisions the leaders made than to any factors in the context. What the pastor did, the style the church took, and the actions of the judicatory made the difference. Let's look at each in turn.

Results of the Pastor's Leadership Style

The founding pastor in a new church development field has incredible power. The tone of ministry he communicates and the style he sets determine, for the most part, who will be attracted to the new congregation. They also largely determine what model the church will follow as it develops. To a lesser degree, the same is true for existing congregations. The pastor's leadership style and tone of ministry greatly influence who, from among the many members, will take an active part in the congregation during his tenure. They also determine what types of new people will be attracted to the congregation, and often, whether the church will grow at all during his ministry. The style of ministry Rick followed in Newton was not only unsuited to the suburb, but was especially unsuited to the development of a new congregation, for a number of reasons.

First, Rick's freewheeling, dynamic, dominating style of ministry attracted people who either were unstable, or were seeking a congregation in which they could be dependent participants. Rick's domineering methods discouraged even those who did have leadership potential from developing it or exercising it. Persons attracted to this congregation, therefore, came primarily, and even exclusively, to have their needs met by the pastor.

One result of gathering an entire congregation on this basis is the lack of available members to assume leadership roles as the congregation grows, and the need for additional leadership increases. No one is available who can be expected to take responsibility, or who is capable of taking responsibility. Those who do assume leadership are often so problem-ridden that they are ineffective.

The fact that Rick's counseling ministry did not encourage membership growth may seem puzzling. Many people who came to him with problems were definitely helped. Why didn't the church grow when so many were being helped?

A therapy style of ministry attracts people needing therapy. Many of those who come to a pastor for counseling have no intention of becoming responsible church members nor are they available to be church participants after they have received the help they need. When they get what they came for, they simply move on. A therapy style of ministry may bring help to a large number of people, but it rarely results in a significant number of church members.

Second, the pastor's own style of ministry, critical of all organization, discouraged the development of needed organization. Rick emphasized one-to-one relationships and built all organizational structure around himself. He was the key communication link between every person and every segment of the congregation. We can illustrate the nature of the church's organization by a simple diagram. The pastor is in the center and all members connect through him.

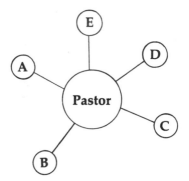

For a very short period during the initial months of a new congregation's life, such an organizational style is appropriate; but the hazards of continuing it are legion. The pastor is the only glue holding the entire organization together. When he leaves, the glue melts and the entire organization disintegrates—that is what happened when Rick left Newton. Every pastor, especially a pastor in a new church, not only needs to encourage others to assume leadership, he actually needs to make room for lay leaders. His access to slots within the organization is so much better, and he often has so much power that he can crowd out even those who actively pursue leadership roles.

Third, another weakness a domineering pastor encourages is the development of a congregation that is too heterogeneous. Rick's leadership style attracted a congregation in which the only common denominator was the members' dependence on him. As people moved into the congregation, there were no natural means for them to interact with other members of the congregation, to determine whether or not they would fit well in the group or have any of their needs met by the group. The result was a congregation composed of an immense variety of individuals, almost completely lacking in social cohesion or integration. When Rick left, the group fell apart, because he was the only thing they had in common.

Fourth, Rick's style of ministry severely stunted the congregation's growth. Church members were attracted to the congregation to be served by him. The congregation was, therefore, effectively limited to the number of persons he could serve.

This limiting factor, inherent in this style of ministry, accounts for the stunted growth of many church development fields in the last two decades. It also explains why ordinary congregations may experience a spurt of growth with the arrival of a new pastor, which then levels off for the balance of his ministry. Growth ceases, because there is a maximum number of people that the pastor's human resources and time enable him to carry.

Fifth, the haphazard, unstable climate of the Newton congregation, while seemingly open to creativity, actually became a poor climate to support innovation. In a congregation with no defined procedures, with very little organizational structure, and with few predictable patterns of life, nearly all energy has to be given over to carrying on the ordinary tasks of life. Everything, even such simple tasks as maintenance of the building, printing material for worship, and so forth, has to be negotiated continually. What at first seems to be an ideal style, open to the creative movements of the spirit, turns out to be a restrictive atmosphere in which the simple tasks of maintaining life on a day-to-day basis consume nearly all the available energy.

Results of the Church Organizational Style

We now turn to factors in the organizational style of the congregation that limited its effectiveness. *The almost complete lack of formal organizational structure is the first of the factors that imposed severe limits on this congregation.*

Where there is no organizational structure, it is very difficult to translate plans into action. When individuals develop creative ideas in a congregation lacking formal organization, there is no structure readily available to implement the ideas. The unwillingness of committee chairpersons to cooperate with those who want to innovate is a common complaint in most congregations. The complainer often fantasizes that life would be much easier if there weren't so many people "in the way." Newton demonstrates that the opposite condition is just as difficult. In this congregation, there was no one in the way; but there was no one in the way because there was no way. The channels of operation were not blocked; they simply did not exist. Everything had to be done on an ad hoc basis. The innovator not only had to develop an idea, but then had to attempt to build a structure through which to implement the idea.

A second organizational factor that limited the effectiveness and the ability of the Newton congregation to grow was its close, intimate fellowship life-style. Rick and others within the congregation often spoke in glowing terms of their close, supportive fellowship. While many of them found this fellowship a meaningful experience in their lives, it was on the whole very inappropriate for the suburban context to which the Newton congregation was attempting to relate.

To most people in the context, the closeness and intimacy of this small congregation made it *in*accessible. It was a social group very difficult for outsiders to break into. In a context where mobility was high, and new people needed social groups that were easy to enter, this congregation seemed to be a group that would be very difficult to enter.

Moreover, becoming a member of this congregation would more than likely prove to be a costly experience for most persons in this highly mobile suburb. Joining this congregation was more akin to getting married or becoming part of a family than joining an organization. Most people in this new suburb are not long-term residents of the area. They expect at some point to have to move on to another location. Most would not choose to make, or would not be capable of making, the human investment necessary to become part of such a close, intimate series of relationships as the Newton congregation presented. One area resident who refused to become a church member was quite specific in giving the church's style as his reason for not joining. He explained that his job required him to move every three or four years. In a previous community, he had invested himself deeply and joined a similar congregation. He said he would never do it again. The cost of leaving, of tearing loose from the deep relationships he had formed, had been too great.

The Newton congregation, because of its style, tended to limit its appeal to those who were more or less stable in the community. Going through its membership rolls indicates that, in fact, these were the kinds of persons it attracted. Unfortunately, there were few persons of this type available in the area interested in becoming part of a congregation, who were not already church members. The appeal of the Newton congregation was, thus, very narrow. It appealed to persons who, for one reason or another, had been in the area for some time, and who either were not attracted to or were unable to sustain a continuing participation in the other congregations serving the same neighborhood—or to those who had needs for counseling, or for forming dependencies, that a domineering minister would meet. The group, gathered in response to the style the Newton congregation exhibited, did not contain sufficient raw material from which to build a strong, stable, ongoing church.

Results of the Regional Judicatory's Role in Newton

The next three factors that we can identify as contributing to the ineffectiveness of the Newton church, center around the role the regional judicatory played.

First, the help the regional judicatory gave the Newton congregation was generally ineffective, because the judicatory executive and consultant accepted both the leadership style and the organizational style of the congregation. As we have already seen, both were major factors limiting the development of the Newton congregation. By affirming the pastor's and congregation's styles as nonnegotiable, these outside resources gave up their ability to provide a needed critique or evaluation of the total ministry and style of the congregation. Instead of helping pastor and congregation to see that they needed to make basic changes, the judicatory consultant ended by affirming the tendencies that were destructive in the congregation.

A second mistake rendering the role of the judicatory ineffective in the Newton congregation was the lack of clear accountability and the lack of a specific definition of the consultant's role. The judicatory executive assumed that all he needed to do was find a consultant who was capable of defining the causes of Newton's decline. He assumed the consultant would then work to solve the problems, and that he could, in effect, turn him loose in the situation to do that. In retrospect, we know that the consultant's definition of Newton's problems and his approach to help the Newton congregation were both erroneous. The muddy definition of his role and the lack of clear accountabilities for his work meant that neither he nor the judicatory discovered his erroneous approach for many months. When the situation did not improve, he simply asked for and received another block of time in which to try to improve the situation, using the precise approaches that were making the situation worse. Newton's example illustrates what is generally true—that a consultant who will work without a clear contract spelling out specific objectives and accountabilities will likely end by, albeit unintentionally, milking his client.

Third, the previous friendship between the judicatory-employed consultant and Pastor Rick probably made the consultant ineffective in this situation. When judicatories and/or congregations face difficult decisions, often an outside consultant can be of immense help. This is especially true when the decision is painful and will deeply effect the lives of those involved. They are often not able to come to terms with reality, when reality means a severe decision, such as the closing of a congregation or the removal of a pastor.

To be effective, the outside consultant must be a true outsider. He must be a disinterested party who can speak the truth in love—that is, with concern for those who are involved—but who is sufficiently detached emotionally that he can indeed speak the truth. The consultant in Newton shied away from making the radical recommendations that needed to be made—namely, that the minister should move and that the congregation should close, because both recommendations seemed such a deep defeat for his friend.

A final observation we can make about the difficulties which beset

Newton revolves around the image of a loser. Once a congregation has developed the image of a loser—that is, a congregation beset with problems—it no longer has the capacity to attract people, especially those who are looking for a congregation that will make a difference in their lives, or through which they can make a difference. Once Newton became clearly identified as "the little church that wouldn't make it," most people around it no longer wanted to be identified with it. If it was going to sink, they didn't want to go down with it.

In summary, the experience of Newton shows us:

1. A pastor who attracts people with problems and who develops dependencies upon himself will find it very difficult to encourage any members to assume leadership responsibility.

2. A pastor who dominates everything in a congregation will end by being indispensable to everything that happens in that congregation. The church will never develop any organization. When he leaves, it will fall apart.

3. A congregation gathered entirely in response to the dominant role of a pastor will not develop social cohesiveness.

4. A congregation gathered entirely in response to the ministry of the founding pastor will be limited in size to the number of persons he can effectively serve.

5. An unstable, haphazard, group climate will discourage innovation.

6. Lack of formal organizational structures in a congregation means there are no structures for action; there are no mechanisms to implement creative ideas.

7. The style of life a congregation develops must be appropriate to the people available to it, or it will not grow.

8. Consultants who do not question the basic style of a congregation or its pastor may miss the fundamental factors rendering a congregation ineffective. They attempt to heal a basic flaw by making only minor adjustments.

9. Lack of clear accountability and specific objectives encourage an ineffective consultant to continue. The result may be a significant waste of resources.

10. Outside consultants need to be truly outsiders, in order to be sufficiently objective to help their clients face up to hard realities.

11. When a congregation develops the image of a loser, it is no longer attractive to many people, especially strong people.

VI. An Old Church Reaches a New Generation

Introduction

After years of steadily losing members, Wilmington Street church begins to attract new members. Neighborhood analysis reveals that new persons, including a surprising number of younger adults, are moving into the city neighborhood the church serves. Sensing a new opportunity, but significant differences in life-style between newcomers and longtime members, the church's planning committee invites a church development consultant to interview the newcomers. His research reveals that key differences do exist; also, that newcomers feel welcome, but not included or integrated into the congregation's core life. The church's planning committee faces the difficult challenge of developing program to meet the different needs of new persons and of planning means for their entry into the life of the congregation.

The Case

Peter Chandler:
I want to commend you as a committee for asking for help to meet an *opportunity*. Most of the time when congregations call me in, it's because they're experiencing difficulty of some kind.

It's refreshing to meet with a group of people who are gathering resources to meet a challenge.

For those of you who haven't had the opportunity to meet me, my name is Peter Chandler. I work in the diocesan office of church planning. I've been here now for two days, primarily to look at your neighborhood firsthand and then to interview some of the new members who have become part of your congregation during the last year and a half.

Before talking about the interviews, I would like to share some of the things your rector and I saw as we drove around your church's neighborhood. As most of you know, the neighborhood is composed largely of two-family houses. That's especially true as you travel down Wilmington Street toward the center of the city. Many of those who live in these houses have lived in the neighborhood for a long time, especially the large number of older people who surround you.

But we also saw many younger adults as we drove around. Some of you probably know that in cities across the country those in the twenty-through-thirty age group are buying property, some out of conviction, some out of necessity. With the average price of a single-family house well in excess of $50,000 these days, most people in this age group can't afford to buy a single-family house in the suburbs. Many of them don't want to compete in the high-pressured suburban society anyway. They prefer the city, with its greater variety of people and wider cultural opportunities.

Also, as we drove around, we were impressed by the large number of people who are improving their houses. Apparently the long trend of neighborhood deterioration is turning around to become a trend of neighborhood improvement. I think we can also take the willingness of these people to invest in their property as an indication that they are making a more permanent commitment to the neighborhood. That's probably why they are interested in your church, as well.

Committee Member (a man in his middle fifties):

Well, we certainly have been pleasantly surprised by the change. After years and years of losing members, all of a sudden we are growing. I've been on and off the vestry for nearly twenty-five years, and I've never seen growth like we're having now. Not that it's sensational, but in the last two years we've had about two dozen new members, and at least half of these are young people in their twenties and early thirties, most of them from the neighborhood.

We asked you to help us because we don't want to miss the opportunity of relating to these new people. Frankly, some of us are as uneasy as we are pleased by their presence. Not that we don't like them. We are friendly enough with them and they with us, but somehow they don't seem part of us yet. I'm not sure we really know how to relate to them—that is, to their needs. Most of us in my generation have had difficulty understanding our own children. While we don't have the same dynamics going between us and our new neighbors as we do in our own families, we still have to face the reality that most of our new neighbors represent a different generation from most of us in this congregation. As much as we want to, I don't think we know how to bridge the gap that both we and they feel. We're hoping that you can give us some insight and some suggestions.

Peter Chandler:

I think you have taken the first major step in your openness. Most of us really think the world is the way we see it, that is, that our view is the accurate view. It's hard for us to admit that the world may, in some respects, be quite different, or that the church also needs to be different from what it was twenty or thirty years ago.

Before we go to any specific suggestions, let's first of all try to understand what has happened over the last two or three decades, and how that's affected people who grew up through these years. That may take a bit of explaining. So please bear with me.

I suppose the first point we need to try to grasp—and you will need to keep a very open mind for the next few minutes—is that the world is *basically* different from the way it was twenty or thirty years ago. In fact, some recent changes are so fundamental that they have disrupted the normal pattern of religious development as most of us who are middle-aged or older experienced it.

For example, we would respond to a concerned mother whose twenty-year-old children have dropped out of church by saying,

105

"They will come around. Just leave them alone, and they'll come back to the church." In the relatively stable or slow-changing society of the past, such advice made good sense. Teen-agers, for generations, have rebelled against their parents and the institutions to which their parents are committed. In the process, they dropped out of church. But sooner or later, usually in their early twenties, often when they married and settled down to the serious business of raising a family, they come back into the fold.

What makes our time so different is the fracturing of this basic pattern. Young and younger middle-aged adults are *not* following in the footsteps of their predecessors. Many of them are no longer marrying. When they do marry, they marry late. Often they do not have children. Even when they do have children, many no longer look to the church for help in raising their children.

The ongoing rapid social change of the present and recent past has given us a society composed of diverse groups of people of various ages whose ways of viewing the world (and the church!) are fundamentally different. This mix of basic viewpoints is the reason why those of us inside the church have such difficulty understanding and communicating with those outside the church. We are by and large of different times and hold different beliefs about what is real and fundamental.

It is difficult to fix precisely the borders between generations. I believe the break is about age forty. When I think about the generation over forty, I think about my own growing up. The over-forty generation is my generation; I am forty-five. Looking around the room tonight, I would say most of us here are in the over-forty generation! What are the fundamental experiences of our generation?

To being with, we are depression children. I was born just after New Year's Day, 1933. The country was in the throes of a terrible economic depression. It was the era of the soup kitchen, the bread line, and the apple seller. It was the bust after the boom. I can still feel the relief and gratitude that my father had a job he would not be likely to lose. I remember how we treasured everything we had, because *everything* was hard-earned.

I remember Pearl Harbor. I remember that Sunday night sitting on the couch and hearing the news accounts. And the next day, I remember the old, brown walnut radio bringing FDR into our home to tell us of the day that would live in infamy.

I remember watching fathers and brothers go to war. Nearly every family was *directly* touched by the war. I remember the desperate feelings of the early war years, when we all knew that the only reason we would win was because God was on our side. I remember VE Day. I was eating breakfast. I remember VJ Day. I was playing outside, and it was hot. In between the two, I remember the feeling of horror as the radio told us of the dropping of one bomb that had brought a fiery death to thousands. Through all those years, I remember the big city church with its seemingly endless pews always full, Sunday after Sunday, its huge choir arranged in theater seats up behind the minister. It felt like Radio City Music Hall. The thought that it would ever close was inconceivable. It would always be there—central and important—like the flag. If you are over forty, probably you can feel all these experiences with me.

If you are under forty, I'll wager you can't. You are of a different generation. Let's try to get in touch with this new generation of adults. I think we over-forty people can understand why so many of them are not in the church, by identifying the very different fundamental experiences of this generation. Their *basic* experience is the fracturing of the fundamental pattern of life I have just outlined. Those fundamental institutions, which my generation and those older fought through war and depression to save, have been seriously broken. This fracturing was never so vivid to me as it was in the summer of 1975, when I met a couple who had not lived in the United States since the mid-sixties. For the past ten years, they had served as missionaries on a primitive field. They had heard only sketchy news reports from the U.S. during those years.

They confronted me with such questions as, "What ever happened to the War on Poverty? Did we win it?" "We've been in the country for two days, and we haven't read about any riots in the cities. Has the lot of black people improved so much that they no longer need to resort to riots to get what they want?"

It was very difficult to answer their questions. I hardly knew where to start. I realized that we had lived through an incredibly difficult era. It was an era in which, as a society, we tried to cope and largely failed. That failure appeared in area after area of life. Many of us lost confidence in the basic institutions of our society. Our government could neither win the War on Poverty nor the war in Vietnam. We came to wonder whether our schools could educate. This was the era of *Why Johnny Can't Read.* We began to doubt our hospitals. George C. Scott made a movie called *Hospital.* Typical was the incident where a woman died in the emergency room, not because they couldn't treat her, but because they forgot about her. The bureaucracy was so cumbersome that nobody noticed she was there; she died of neglect. Even the family seemed on the brink of collapse as the divorce rate climbed to one in three marriages. On and on the list goes, including, finally, the church. A major magazine article of the time was called, "The Most Wasted Hour of the Week." The article was about the Sunday school. And those of us who, like myself, are chronic religious participators, watched a 50 percent drop in church school participation in the face of an equally increasing number of children in the population eligible to attend Sunday school. We saw a similar experience in adult participation. Adults dropped out of the church by the thousands, mostly younger to middle-aged adults. The median age of those who continued to participate in the church steadily rose.

Many people's basic beliefs changed during these years. Large segments of the adult population came to believe that a person can be adequate, good, even religious, without having anything to do with the church. Many people began to view the church at best as optional—at worst, as an ineffective or even hypocritical institution. Today we are surrounded by this subculture, composed mainly of younger adults, but taking in many sympathizers who see the world pretty much as these younger adults see it. This segment of our society has grown up largely apart from the church, though that doesn't necessarily mean its members are not religious. They may avoid institutional religion, but we misread them if we believe they have no interest in religion at all.

Insurance Broker (in his late fifties, well-dressed, obviously successful):

Well, it certainly is good to see that these young people are finally coming around! I've always believed that sooner or later they would come back to church—when they grew up, or things got tough.

Peter Chandler:

Well, those may not be the only or even the main reasons they are beginning to return. My purpose in attempting to clarify differences in the overall social experiences of the two generations, and those who identify with each, is to highlight what is involved when we middle-aged church members attempt to communicate with many of the present outsiders. We usually approach them by attempting to recall them to the church, or at least to point out to them what we believe is obviously valuable, meaningful, necessary about the church. In my opinion, this approach, which has traditionally been effective, is inherently doomed to failure with the present outsiders. We are trying to recall them to the church on the basis of fundamental experiences and convictions which we have had, but which they have never had. They have never seen a government that can cope, an army that can win, a school that can educate, or a church that has made a real difference in people's lives.

We say to them, "You really ought to give it a try." They wonder, "Why?" When we offer all our explanations about its importance or its effectiveness, they seem to these outsiders to have no basis in reality at all. Many are still profoundly disillusioned with themselves and with the church. Even as they now turn to the church, they are still angry that it let them down when it refused to confront the great moral issues of the sixties.

For example, drawing from the research I just completed with your newest members, I interviewed a young woman who is a "child of the sixties." She grew up in a small town, then left to attend a large state university, just as the social activism of that era was sweeping college campuses. A sensitive person with intense moral concern, she quickly fell into the movement. The causes of social justice seemed to her much more critical to attend to than going to school, so she left college. She went to

109

work for a lawyer in the Civil Liberties Union, defending poor blacks in Alabama. She was horrified at the injustices these people suffered and equally horrified that her parents and their friends back in her hometown refused to believe her when she told them how unfair our American system of justice was. The clinching blow came when she left her husband, because he allowed himself to be drafted to fight the war in Vietnam. "I said to him, 'Run away, hide, go to Canada, go to jail; do anything, but don't fight in this immoral war!' But he refused to listen, so I left him. I saw the overall bases of our lives were totally different." Needless to say, her Second-World-War-bred parents were dismayed to the point of nearly disowning her.

"To this day, they don't understand why I had to do what I did," she told me. "In fact, no one who didn't grow up through the horror of those years can really appreciate what we went through."

Committee member:

I'm beginning to understand what this "generation gap" is all about, but I'm also really frustrated! How in the world are we ever going to appeal to these people who are not only outside the church, but most of whom have had no experience with the church, and many of whom feel negatively about it?"

Peter Chandler:

I'm afraid I have no simple answer to your question, but I do have some suggestions about getting started. I think that we will begin to touch the present generation of outsiders only as we speak to *their* experience. I think they will relate openly to us insofar as they believe we understand and appreciate them. I believe they will feel that we appreciate and understand them only when we really do—and that will take lots of reaching out and lots of listening. Now, there are some ways to do that, some strategies which may be helpful. I'm going to suggest a couple in a minute, but I need to emphasize that we dare not treat these strategies as gimmicks. As we act, we need to act out of authentic caring. If we are not authentic, we will be found out.

Six months ago, I visited another church located in a neighborhood similar to yours. I made some suggestions to them which they have followed. I would like to share the results. In fact,

110

I have a letter from their rector with me; and I will read it after I tell you what I suggested to them.

Their congregation, like yours, has many members who no longer live in the neighborhood right around the church. When I asked them how many people they could call by name who live in houses in the blocks immediately around the church building, most of them could name only a handful. It seemed to me that they needed to get reacquainted with the neighborhood in which their church is located, and especially that they needed to get to know the new people moving in.

I suggested a very simple strategy. I said, "Why don't you take a block at a time, knock on every front door and invite the people who live in that house to have supper with you at your church the following Sunday evening. If a dozen of your church members are willing to bring the food, something like a potluck supper with enough extra food for the church's neighbors, I'll wager that the evening will build immense openness on the part of your neighbors toward the congregation. You will get to know some of the new neighbors, and you might even find some new people who will be interested in participating in your congregation. I wouldn't try to recruit anybody on that evening—just welcome them."

Well, they did it! I want to read to you their rector's description of what happened.

Last Sunday night, we held a block supper for people in our immediate neighborhood. The Sunday night before, about eight people went out and knocked on doors and extended an invitation to come for supper. We explained that the purpose of the supper was for us to get to know our neighbors, for them to get to know each other, and for us to hear any suggestions they might have as to how we could better serve our community.

Amazingly, thirty-three people accepted our initial invitation. We called them back later that week to remind them of the supper, and the number held at thirty-three. The night of the supper, however, only thirteen actually showed up; and we had twelve members from the church.

In spite of our disappointment with the attendance, this turned out to be a good night. At the initiative of our guests, it became much more of a church-oriented experience than we had planned for. They wanted to know about the church and wanted a tour of the facilities. We even had an impromptu mini-recital on the organ. We may have gained two new families from the experience. The whole thing turned out much differently than any of us had anticipated.

Our guests expressed a great deal of appreciation for this particular effort, and there is no doubt that we generated a great deal of goodwill among those who attended. Because of this, the committee will probably consider doing more of these kinds of neighborhood programs in the future.

I am sharing this experience with you tonight because it fits your situation so well. When I ask your new members, "What attracts you to this congregation?" hardly any of them mention program. They mention people. Many of them mention by name a particular church member who has reached out and befriended them. The city can be a lonely place, especially when you are new and have only a few friends. For that reason, anyone who reaches out to you becomes a very important person in your life.

So I think the first step you need to take is to consciously develop strategies to communicate your genuine caring more intentionally to those around you. Then as new persons respond and eventually grow comfortable with you, you can begin to plan *with them* program to meet their particular needs. Program which will meet their needs, by the way, will probably be different from any program you now have. Most church groups are formed to meet the needs of a particular social group. Then they grow up with that social group. A new generation or another social group tends to have different needs and demands a different group program to relate to those needs. The delicate task you face, if you want to integrate new people into your congregation, is to find ways to give them access to your resources and to plan with them program and organization which *they* find helpful.

Those inside a congregation hold the keys that new people need to enter. If you want new people to enter your congregation, *you* have to make it possible for them to enter. If you want them to come all the way into your congregation, you have to make it possible for them to enter into the core of your life. That means reaching out as you are already doing, but it also means including the new people in the center of the congregation's decision-making. It means giving them access to your resources and building with them a church that is for them.

What We Can Learn from Wilmington Street

A new era is emerging for many older congregations. For the first time in several decades, changes in the neighborhoods around them are favorable. The moving forces behind these changes, as Peter Chandler indicated, stem from both shifts in values and changing economics. For many younger adults especially, the suburban dream is no longer as attractive as it was a generation ago. They are not pleased with the suburban attitude toward life, especially values that find expression in suburban "gracious living." Many do not believe they can attain an economic base sufficient to support an affluent suburban life-style. Job opportunities are increasingly limited, a trend that, according to most economic indicators, is likely to worsen. The years ahead will be leaner.

City neighborhoods, as well as some rural areas, represent an attractive alternative both in terms of values and economics. Housing is available much more reasonably. The heterogeneous environment of the city with its mix of age groups, social groups, and ethnic groups, as well as its variety of social and cultural opportunities, is much more appealing than sharply stratified and often socially segregated suburban neighborhoods. In many cities, urban renewal agencies stand ready to provide funds to those willing to invest themselves in the task of renovating their property, in the form of either outright grants or low interest loans. These economic and social changes offer new opportunities to city neighborhoods and a growing number of rural congregations.

But these opportunities will become reality only in those congregations that are able to change. Most city congregations were established during the last century to serve constituents who then lived in the neighborhood immediately around the church building. As these constituents have moved up the economic ladder and out to the suburbs, city neighborhood congregations have increasingly been supported by members who grew up in the neighborhood around them, but who now live some distance away and who, out of loyalty, drive back to support the old church. Their long service and economic position favor these nonresident members who consequently usually dominate the old church. As a result, its program is shaped to meet their needs much more than the needs of new persons moving into the neighborhood. Some rural congregations whose areas lost population to suburban migration are now surrounded with younger adults seeking a simpler, less costly life-style. But they too are usually dominated by lifelong members who often find the newcomers difficult to accept.

As these neighborhoods recover, their churches' renewal depends on the willingness of those who presently dominate them to help reshape them. Only as these socially isolated congregations build some bridges, can they relate effectively to those who now live in their neighborhoods. Specifically, what does that task involve?

First, present church leaders need to recognize that the generation gap is real. Speaking to a large gathering, Margaret Mead described the gap in an imaginary dialogue between parents and their children.

The parents say to their children, "Someday when you grow up and have more experience, you will see that the world really is the way we say it is."

The children respond to the parents, "You have never been young in the way we are young."

The impasse in this dialogue stems from the fact that both are right in terms of their respective generations. In the process of growing up, all of us have certain basic experiences that provide filters through which we view the world for the rest of our lives. In the case we have just considered, Peter Chandler made this point when he described the over-forty and under-forty generations. During most of human history, the ordinary process of maturing presented little difficulty—other than the normal amount of conflict between parents and their children. The world changed very slowly. The social experiences of each generation were very similar to those of the previous generation. However, in this time of rapid social change, the world itself really is radically different from generation to generation. The generation gap is real.

In addition to the generation gap, rapid social change produces another gap which I term a social gap. We can understand what this social gap is and the complexity to which it leads, by looking at its impact on institutions. Institutions tend to be inherently conservative; they give places of honor or power to those who are older or more experienced. Traditionally, in the slowly changing world, this was the wisest course of action. However, now the world changes rapidly and radically. Those who hold power view the world through determinative experiences which are no longer generally valid, or which are radically different from the determinative experiences of most of those around them. Their peculiar set of experiences differentiates them and forms a social gap between them and other social groups. The needs they have or had, the policies or programs they find meaningful, are not necessarily helpful or meaningful to the emerging generation, or to social groups different from themselves. Unless they are unusually perceptive, their particular world view leads them to make the false assumption that the world at large truly is as they see it, and *not* as it is viewed by others.

Those who hold positions of power in the church control, either openly or subtly, the kinds of people who will enter the church. A major hurdle today's church insiders need to overcome, in order to attract new groups, is within themselves. As long as they view outsiders or new people, even subtly, as immature or bad, they will find it very difficult to relate helpfully to them. In reality, outsiders and new people are neither bad nor immature. They are simply different.

Second, to relate to its neighborhood, the socially isolated church needs to reestablish its presence in that neighborhood. It comes as a surprise to most active church members to discover that most new people really are not aware of what a local church does. In most cases, its life and activity are far from obvious. One typical city neighborhood resident I interviewed can speak for many. He lives across the street from a church. He watched the church for some time from the *front*. It didn't seem to him anything was ever going on. Later on, when he joined the church, he was quite surprised to learn how much activity occurred at the church during the week. He pointed out that most people who attend activities at his church drive there and park in the church parking lot, located in *back* of the church. It's not obvious to neighborhood people that anything is going on, because they can't see anyone going in or or out. The parking lot is entered from a side street.

When the predominant group served by a church is socially exclusive, or nonresident, it needs to develop some strategy similar to Wilmington Street's potluck suppers. Such a strategy establishes the important fact that the church is there to serve all the people who now live in the neighborhood, and not just the constituency who drive in, or those who have always lived there.

A third necessity when the church is facing new people is the establishment of different program to serve the different needs of the new people.

To begin this task, the church must break the assumption of the longstanding members that program which they find meaningful will meet the needs of most newcomers, if only they will give it a chance. Such is not likely to happen. Most church organizations are created for a specific purpose. People who are concerned about that purpose form a group. However, as time passes, the emphasis of the organization usually shifts from program to social. Social interaction within the organization becomes as meaningful, and sometimes more meaningful to its members, as the purpose for which the organization was originally founded. The organization may even retain a name that describes its original purpose, but carry on activities that are completely different.

The more the organization is characterized as a social group, the more difficult it becomes for new people to penetrate it. Newcomers who attend meetings, thinking the organization will be what its name says it is, and who then discover it does not do what its name implies it does, are often disappointed. Longstanding members, on the other hand, who attend as much to be with each other as for the purpose of the organization, find it difficult to understand the disappointment of the new person. They generally fail to appreciate how deeply the organization is intertwined with longstanding social relationships, which the new person lacks. It is important for longstanding members to recognize that church organizations grow up with particular generations and specific social groups. A new generation or social group requires new program and usually, new structures to carry that program.

We now turn to positive steps churches can take to make contact with outsiders.

The first step is simply to offer sincere caring to outsiders. Initially, outsiders were much more impressed with the genuine caring extended to them by the Wilmington Street congregation than they were with *any* of its program. Recent new members indicated they came to this church out of basic loneliness. Living in the city can be a lonely experience, especially for new people. Many of those who joined Wilmington Street spoke of their neighborhoods as unfriendly, cold, at times even hostile. They were very grateful for the friendship that church members offered them. Some indicated the church was the only institution they had contact with week by week which offered free acceptance.

A close examination of those who offer friendship to outsiders at Wilmington Street reveals that surprisingly few church members are involved. In the interviews Peter Chandler conducted, newcomers mentioned people who have reached out to them *by name.* However, the list of names is very short; the same few people are mentioned again and again. One strategy churches can follow to attract more people is simply to encourage more of their members to share themselves genuinely and openly with strangers who visit their congregations.

A second strategy that will draw new members is to bring newcomers into the heart of the congregation's program planning. As we have already noted, current church members hold in their hands the means of access to the church's resources. If new people are going to have access to the church's resources, it will have to be given to them by the members currently in power.

Granting access will probably not come easily. More than likely, newcomers will not actually be admitted to positions of power until the church board makes a formal policy decision, providing spaces for new people, as well as for longstanding members, and also apportions some of the church's resources to program specifically aimed at the needs of the newcomers.

New members interviewed at Wilmington Street indicate they feel attracted to and welcomed by the congregation, but generally do not feel included. They feel socially distant from longstanding members, and they feel they are on the edges of the church structure and program. They need to be brought into the core life of the congregation. They will feel welcome, but they will not feel truly included in this congregation until they are, in fact, admitted to seats of influence.

Such a step is not easy for longstanding members to take. It involves spending the church's resources for program that they do not find personally meaningful, and that probably will never seem to them as important or critical as programs they have supported for many years. But the investment is essential. While warmth attracts new persons, it takes program to hold them—program that speaks to their needs.

Finally, incorporating newcomers into the life of a congregation also involves reaching out to and including the newcomers' social groups. In older congregations, especially, most longstanding members count many of their close friends among members of the congregation. In the interviews Peter Chandler conducted with new members at Wilmington Street, he asked, "Are your two best friends members of this church, members of another church or not active in any church?" Only one person indicated that one of her friends was a member of the Wilmington Street congregation!

Program that speaks specifically to the needs of the newcomers probably will speak also to the needs of their friends. A congregation that invests in the development of such program is in a position to relate to new networks of persons, far beyond its immediate neighborhood. Most people today live as much within social networks as they do in their immediate neighborhoods. Newcomers and their close friends will have similar needs and interests. The congregation now will not be limited only to its neighborhood, or former residents of that neighborhood, but can relate to entirely new social groups. Newcomers whose needs are met by the church may then see their friends within these social networks as potential church members. If their experience with the church is meaningful, they are likely to believe it also can be meaningful for their friends.

Breaking down social barriers in order to relate to new groups is never an easy task. Wilmington Street has made a significant beginning. A congregation that becomes aware of the reasons it is attracting outsiders can consciously encourage and support its current members in following strategies to enhance that appeal. But unless it also takes steps to integrate new members into its core life, it will more than likely lose its capacity to appeal to new groups.

In summary, we can identify several strategies a congregation can employ to relate to a new social group and to open the way for them to become part of its ongoing life.

1. Recognize that the social gap between existing church members and new people is real, and that existing members hold most of the power to bridge it.

2. When a new social group moves into a congregation's immediate neighborhood, the congregation needs to reestablish its visibility and presence with the new group.

3. Existing church organizations are likely to be pertinent to insiders, but not to outsiders. More than likely, a congregation will need to develop different program and different church groups to meet the needs of new people.

4. Opening the way for new people to enter a congregation is initially a matter of genuine, open caring.

5. New members will not feel included in a congregation

119

until existing church members include them formally in the process of program planning, and allocate resources to support program which meets the new members' needs. Warmth attracts; program holds.

6. Church leaders can appeal through initial newcomers to others within their networks of relationships.

VII. The Challenge of Leadership in a Time of Change

The six cases we have just studied provide a laboratory of insight into the challenges of church leadership in our time. In this short summary chapter, I want to point up overall insights which emerge from the cases. I shall begin with general principles of leadership which these cases reconfirm, and then turn to some leadership skills especially critical in our time of rapid social change.

First, the general principles:

1. *Begin well*. The first few months of a new pastorate, of a new congregation, after a new program is established, when a congregation changes its direction, or when churches change their structure, are *always* critical. Impressions made, habits established, attitudes encouraged, and structures developed will probably determine the shape of the congregation's life for years to come.

2. *Honor the context*. Social and economic factors that operate in the community or neighborhood in which a congregation is situated exert more influence and set more limits on the congregation's life than any other single set of factors. Persons present in the context, and available to the congregation, set

limits on types of program which can be successful in that congregation. Their values, attitudes, and needs set limits on the type of ministry that will be effective in that context. A pastor and congregation who wish to thrive in a given context must shape their style to be appropriate to that context.

3. *Establish good communication.* Good communication within and among churches conveys accurate information and gives an opportunity to correct misinformation. It provides open channels from leaders to the church's membership and from the church's membership to the leaders, as well as among church members. It is as necessary to the healthy function of a congregation as the circulatory system is to a human body.

4. *Deal promptly and positively with conflict.* Conflict is a normal experience in congregational life. When conflict occurs, however, it demands immediate attention. Conflict that is not attended to immediately is like a neglected infection, and sooner or later it will engulf the entire organization.

5. *Build a positive church image.* The image a congregation impresses upon its community determines the types of persons who will be attracted to it. A congregation that appears to be a loser, or to be ingrown, or to be exclusive, is likely to be unable to make the broad appeal necessary to enable it to thrive.

We turn now to principles of leadership that carry heightened importance in our time of rapid change:

1. *No congregation is self-sufficient anymore.* Our world experiences so much change and is so complex that *no* congregation, whatever its resources, has the capacity to meet all the program demands of all persons within and around it. Turning to others for help must become a natural and common experience.

2. *Change is a threatening experience.* This is especially true for weaker congregations, for whom most changes in the last several decades have been negative. Needed innovations within these congregations should be introduced slowly and tenderly. Pastors, as well as churches, generally find change difficult when it affects them directly.

3. *To increase a congregation's relevance, empower "the outsiders."* Positions of power within most congregations are held by

longstanding members who have a natural bias toward the past. When a congregation needs to close the social and generation gaps, it can do so most easily by admitting to positions of power those who represent new social groups and a new generation. There they can act directly to broaden the congregation's life.

4. *It requires persistence to establish innovation.* A new structure or a new set of procedures or a new program seems to be an imposition to a congregation, in much the same manner a new routine feels awkward to an individual. Only with the passing of time does any innovation become natural. It usually takes years to penetrate deeply enough into church members' experience to be routine.

5. *Avoid fostering strong personal dependencies.* People cannot break free of strong dependencies easily, once they are established. Innovative programs, especially, tend to be identified with the leaders who establish them. Leaders themselves need to be aware of this fact and help church members fairly soon to draw their resources from a number of sources including one another.

6. *External accountability keeps people working at difficult tasks.* Often the regular return of an outside consultant or resource person is sufficient to encourage local leaders to complete tasks they might otherwise neglect.

7. *Prompt action is essential.* Some opportunities are fleeting—for example, reaching a new social group moving into an old neighborhood, or developing a cooperative program structure among several congregations, when pastoral leadership posts are unfilled. To delay may mean to miss the opportunity altogether. The stewardship of timeliness is an important one.

8. *Organizational change can be very costly to people.* As church organizations change, it is important to give careful attention to what happens to all persons caught up in the process. Leaders need to be especially attuned to the interests of weaker and less vocal persons who will not advocate for themselves.

9. *The same change may benefit some and hurt others.* A new program which some find helpful may simply be an added burden to others. A new structure that makes church work

easier for some may make participation more difficult for others.

10. *There is a limit to the social diversity a congregation can contain.* A congregation can accept all people, but there are limits to the variety of people for whom it can adequately provide program. Every congregation needs to make its program choices carefully and consciously, because the program it chooses to develop will set limits on the types of persons it attracts.

Practical help in developing and administering a more effective church program

Creative Leadership Series
Lyle E. Schaller, editor. Paper

_____Assimilating New Members by Lyle E. Schaller 01938-9, $3.95

_____Beginning a New Pastorate by Robert G. Kemper 02750-0, $3.95

_____The Care and Feeding of Volunteers by Douglas W. Johnson 04669-6, $3.95

_____Time Management by Speed B. Leas 42120-9 $3.95

_____Creative Stewardship by Richard B. Cunningham 09844-0, $4.95

_____Your Church Can Be Healthy by C. Peter Wagner 46870-1, $4.95

_____Building an Effective Youth Ministry by Glenn E. Ludwig 16300-5, $4.95

_____Leading Churches Through Change by Douglas Alan Walrath 21270-7, $4.95

Mail entire page to:

Customer Service Manager, Abingdon, 201 Eighth Avenue South, Nashville, TN 37202

Please send the books checked above.
I am enclosing $_____(plus 35¢ to cover postage and handling).
Please send check or money order—no cash or C.O.D. accepted.

Name _____
                        (Please print or type)
Address_____

City_____ State_____Zip_____

Please allow three weeks for delivery.